WAR
POEMS

WAR POEMS

AN ANTHOLOGY OF UNFORGETTABLE VERSE

EDITED BY
BRIAN BUSBY

ARCTURUS

For
Edward Maurice Busby
Canadian Overseas Expeditionary Force
(1914–1918)

ARCTURUS

This edition published in 2010 by Arcturus Publishing Limited
26/27 Bickels Yard, 151–153 Bermondsey Street,
London SE1 3HA

ISBN: 978-1-84837-573-4
AD001463EN

Printed in the UK

CONTENTS

INTRODUCTION

Any mention of war poetry invariably brings with it images of the soldier poet, that heroic soul committing verse to paper, creating art through human need and emotion. A romantic, partly fanciful figure, with a few exceptions, he is not to be found in the better part of literary history. Among the earliest writers of English language war poetry we find names like John Milton, Andrew Marvell and William Davenant. These men, fortunate in birth, were raised in comfortable circumstances and blessed with a classical education. There was fighting to be done, but they did not participate. War was for them distant, foreign and, more often than not, it encouraged outpourings of loyalty, often accompanied by idealized, unrealistic depictions of battle.

All changed in the 19th century, most evident in the wealth of poetry written during the American Civil War. While the most accomplished verse of that conflict was produced by Walt Whitman, Herman Melville, Emily Dickinson and others who did not serve in combat, for the first time we find a great number of poems composed by the soldiers themselves. The slow, steady rise in literacy goes only some way towards explaining this significant break. More important, perhaps, is the advent of the citizen soldier. Most who fought and died in the American Civil War had had no previous military experience; they were anything but professional soldiers. W. S. Hawkins was a student, Daniel Bedinger Lucas practiced law and Ambrose Bierce, the most skilled soldier-poet of the conflict, was a newspaperman.

We see this pattern repeat, on a much smaller scale, in much smaller conflicts, during the Boer Wars. Here we have literary giants Rudyard Kipling and Thomas Hardy writing of a conflict that popular writer Edgar Wallace and physician John McCrae experienced and recorded to greater effect.

As the author of 'In Flanders Fields', McCrae is more closely identified with the First World War, the conflict in which the soldier-poet is dominant.

True, Kipling and the elderly Hardy were still producing work of significance, but both pale beside much of the verse that grew in the muddy, rat infested, carcass-ridden trenches of France and Belgium. Some, such as the immortal Wilfred Owen, entered the conflict thinking themselves poets, but many more became so out of a simple desire for expression. They found devoted followers through the pages of magazines and daily newspapers; the work of nearly one thousand was set in type. The more prolific produced collections of verse – rarely more than one, frequently padded with letters and journal entries, often published posthumously.

While not all of the First World War soldier-poets died in the conflict, it can be argued that the greater number of the very finest perished. Rupert Brooke was felled by blood poisoning, the result of a mosquito bite. A German shell killed Edward Thomas. Isaac Rosenberg, a sickly man, died a horrible death in hand-to-hand combat. And, at the end of this long cortège, we find Owen, caught in machine gun fire one week before the Armistice.

Owen's friend and mentor, Siegfried Sassoon, survived the war, as did Robert Graves, while others arrived home lesser men. Ivor Gurney, who is only now beginning to receive the recognition he deserves, managed to struggle on for four more years before succumbing to mental illness.

It is right to be disappointed by what has followed. The War to End All Wars has proven itself to be anything but. Its horrors – the gas, the rats, the disease – fairly pale beside the ovens of Auschwitz and the shadows of Hiroshima and Nagasaki.

That said, it seems perverse to feel let down by the relatively small amount of truly great war verse that these last nine decades have inspired. While acknowledging the accomplished verse inspired by the American Civil War and the Boer Wars, we see now that the soldier-poets of the First World War were not following a well-worn path, nor were they establishing a tradition.

Seven decades ago, this was not so clear. Amongst the death, destruction and deprivation of the Second World War, it was expected that a new flowering of war poets would come. The question was posed: 'Where are the war poets?' Indeed, C. Day-Lewis, who served in the Home Guard, used this very query as the title of a poem first published in February 1941, a mere seventeen months into the conflict.

In response, one might rightly say, where were the readers? In the twenty years, nine months and nineteen days between the first and second World Wars much had changed. Poetry, so very much appreciated in the reigns of Victoria, Edward VII and, to some extent, George V, had taken a lesser place to the novel, radio and movies. This is not to say that no poems of significance were written about the war. One very sad fact about the Second World War is that its greatest English-language soldier-poets died in early age. Keith Douglas was killed in his twenty-fifth year, Sidney Keyes had only just turned twenty-one. Alun Lewis, the eldest, was twenty-eight years old when he died.

The Second World War gave birth to a number of accomplished novels, such as *Brideshead Revisited* and *From Here to Eternity*, along with films like *Casablanca* and *Mrs Miniver*. So, too, did America's war in Vietnam; yet even the greatest literature of that conflict, works like Tim O'Brien's *The Things They Carried*, Michael Herr's *Dispatches*, and *Dien Cai Dau* by Yusef Komunyakaa, lie well within the shadows cast by the popularity of films like *The Deer Hunter*, *The Killing Fields*, *Full Metal Jacket* and *Apocalypse, Now!* Simply put, poetry commands neither the attention nor the place of prominence it once did.

The poetry in this collection reaches from John Donne's 'The Burnt Ship', inspired by a 1596 navel expedition against Spain, to 'Here, Bullet', written by Brian Turner, a United States Army veteran who served in Iraq. This span of more than four centuries encompasses work that demonstrates valour, glory, horror, sorrow and shame. Each contributes to our understanding of war.

Where are the war poets? They are with us still. Perhaps the question we should be asking ourselves is why so little attention is being paid.

Brian Busby
Saint Marys, Ontario

THE GATHERING STORM

Beat! beat! drums! – Blow! bugles! blow!
Through the windows – through doors – burst like a ruthless force,
Into the solemn church, and scatter the congregation;
Into the school where the scholar is studying . . .

The Soldier Going to the Field

Preserve thy sighs, unthrifty girl,
    To purify the air;
Thy tears to thread, instead of pearl,
    On bracelets of thy hair.

The trumpet makes the echo hoarse,
    And wakes the louder drum;
Expense of grief gains no remorse
    When sorrow should be dumb:

For I must go where lazy Peace
    Will hide her drowsy head,
And, for the sport of kings, increase
    The number of the dead.

But first I'll chide thy cruel theft:
    Can I in war delight
Who, being of my heart bereft,
Can have no heart to fight?

Thou know'st the sacred laws of old
    Ordained a thief should pay,

To quit him of his theft, sevenfold
What he had stol'n away.

Thy payment shall but double be:
O then with speed resign
My own seduced heart to me
Accompanied with thine.

William Davenant

* * *

To Lucasta, Going to the Wars

Tell me not, Sweet, I am unkind,
That from the nunnery
Of thy chaste breast and quiet mind
To war and arms I fly.

True, a new mistress now I chase,
The first foe in the field;
And with a stronger faith embrace
A sword, a horse, a shield.

Yet this inconstancy is such
As thou too shalt adore;

I could not love thee, Dear, so much,
Loved I not Honour more.

Richard Lovelace

* * *

Song

Written at Sea in the First Dutch War, 1665,
the Night Before an Engagement

To all you ladies now at land,
We men at sea indite;
But first would have you understand
How hard it is to write:
The Muses now, and Neptune, too,
We must implore to write to you.

For tho' the Muses should prove kind,
And fill our empty brain,
Yet, if rough Neptune rouse the wind
To rouse the azure main,
Our paper, pen, and ink, and we,
Roll up and down our ships at sea.

Then if we write not by each post,
    Think not we are unkind;
Nor yet conclude our ships are lost
    By Dutchmen or by wind:
Our tears we'll send a speedier way,
The tide shall bring them twice a day.

The King, with wonder and surprise
    Will swear the seas grow bold,
Because the tides will higher rise
    Than e'er they did of old:
But let him know it is our tears
Bring floods of grief to Whitehall stairs.

Should foggy Opdam chance to know
    Our sad and dismal story,
The Dutch would scorn so weak a foe,
    And say they've gained no glory:
For what resistance can they find
From men who've left their hearts behind?

Let wind and weather do its worst,
    Be you to us but kind;

Let Dutchmen vapour, Spaniards curse,
No sorrow we shall find:
'Tis then no matter how things go,
Or who's our friend, or who's our foe.

To pass our tedious hours away,
We throw a merry main,
Or else at serious ombre play;
But why should we in vain
Each other's ruin thus pursue?
We were undone when we left you.

But now our fears tempestuous grow
And cast our hopes away,
Whilst you, regardless of our woe,
Sit careless at a play:
Perhaps permit some happier man
To kiss your hand, or flirt your fan.

When any mournful tune you hear,
That dies in every note,
As if it sighed with each man's care
For being so remote,

Think then how often love we've made
To you, when all those tunes were played.

In justice you cannot refuse
    To think of our distress,
When we for hopes of honour lose
    Our certain happiness;
All those designs are but to prove
Ourselves more worthy of your love.

And now we've told you all our loves,
    And likewise all our fears,
In hopes this declaration moves
    Some pity for our tears:
Let's hear of no inconstancy,
We have too much of that at sea.

Charles Sackville

* * *

FEARS IN SOLITUDE

A green and silent spot, amid the hills,
A small and silent dell! O'er stiller place
No singing skylark ever poised himself.
The hills are healthy, save that swelling slope,
Which hath a gay and gorgeous covering on,
All golden with the never-bloomless furze,
Which now blooms most profusely: but the dell,
Bathed by the mist, is fresh and delicate
As vernal cornfield, or the unripe flax,
When, through its half-transparent stalks, at eve,
The level sunshine glimmers with green light.
Oh! 'tis a quiet spirit-healing nook!
Which all, methinks, would love; but chiefly he,
The humble man, who, in his youthful years,
Knew just so much of folly, as had made
His early manhood more securely wise!
Here he might lie on fern or withered heath,
While from the singing lark (that sings unseen
The minstrelsy that solitude loves best),
And from the sun, and from the breezy air,
Sweet influences trembled o'er his frame;

And he, with many feelings, many thoughts,
Made up a meditative joy, and found
Religious meanings in the forms of Nature!
And so, his senses gradually wrapt
In a half sleep, he dreams of better worlds,
And dreaming hears thee still, O singing lark,
That singest like an angel in the clouds!
       My God! it is a melancholy thing
For such a man, who would full fain preserve
His soul in calmness, yet perforce must feel
For all his human brethren – O my God!
It weighs upon the heart, that he must think
What uproar and what strife may now be stirring
This way or that way o'er these silent hills –
Invasion, and the thunder and the shout,
And all the crash of onset; fear and rage,
And undetermined conflict – even now,
Even now, perchance, and in his native isle:
Carnage and groans beneath this blessed sun!
We have offended, Oh! my countrymen!
We have offended very grievously,
And been most tyrannous. From east to west
A groan of accusation pierces Heaven!

The wretched plead against us; multitudes
Countless and vehement, the sons of God,
Our brethren! Like a cloud that travels on,
Steamed up from Cairo's swamps of pestilence,
Even so, my countrymen! have we gone forth
And borne to distant tribes slavery and pangs,
And, deadlier far, our vices, whose deep taint
With slow perdition murders the whole man,
His body and his soul! Meanwhile, at home,
All individual dignity and power
Engulfed in Courts, Committees, Institutions,
Associations and Societies,
A vain, speech-mouthing, speech-reporting Guild,
One Benefit-Club for mutual flattery,
We have drunk up, demure as at a grace,
Pollutions from the brimming cup of wealth;
Contemptuous of all honourable rule,
Yet bartering freedom and the poor man's life
For gold, as at a market! The sweet words
Of Christian promise, words that even yet
Might stem destruction, were they wisely preached,
Are muttered o'er by men, whose tones proclaim
How flat and wearisome they feel their trade;

Rank scoffers some, but most too indolent
To deem them falsehoods or to know their truth.
Oh! blasphemous! the Book of Life is made
A superstitious instrument, on which
We gabble o'er the oaths we mean to break;
For all must swear – all and in every place,
College and wharf, council and justice-court;
All, all must swear, the briber and the bribed,
Merchant and lawyer, senator and priest,
The rich, the poor, the old man and the young;
All, all make up one scheme of perjury,
That faith doth reel; the very name of God
Sounds like a juggler's charm; and, bold with joy,
Forth from his dark and lonely hiding-place,
(Portentious sight!) the owlet Atheism,
Sailing on obscene wings athwart the noon,
Drops his blue-fringéd lids, and holds them close,
And hooting at the glorious sun in Heaven,
Cries out, 'Where is it?'
       Thankless too for peace,
(Peace long preserved by fleets and perilous seas)
Secure from actual warfare, we have loved
To swell the war-whoop, passionate for war!

Alas! for ages ignorant of all
Its ghastlier workings, (famine or blue plague,
Battle, or siege, or flight through wintry snows),
We, this whole people, have been clamorous
For war and bloodshed; animating sports,
The which we pay for as a thing to talk of,
Spectators and not combatants! No guess
Anticipative of a wrong unfelt,
No speculation on contingency,
However dim and vague, too vague and dim
To yield a justifying cause; and forth,
(Stuffed out with big preamble, holy names,
And adjurations of the God in Heaven,)
We send our mandates for the certain death
Of thousands and ten thousands! Boys and girls,
And women, that would groan to see a child
Pull off an insect's wing, all read of war,
The best amusement for our morning meal!
The poor wretch, who has learnt his only prayers
From curses, and who knows scarcely words enough
To ask a blessing from his Heavenly Father,
Becomes a fluent phraseman, absolute
And technical in victories and defeats,

And all our dainty terms for fratricide;
Terms which we trundle smoothly o'er our tongues
Like mere abstractions, empty sounds to which
We join no feeling and attach no form!
As if the soldier died without a wound;
As if the fibres of this godlike frame
Were gored without a pang; as if the wretch,
Who fell in battle, doing bloody deeds,
Passed off to Heaven, translated and not killed;
As though he had no wife to pine for him,
No God to judge him! Therefore, evil days
Are coming on us, O my countrymen!
And what if all-avenging Providence,
Strong and retributive, should make us know
The meaning of our words, force us to feel
The desolation and the agony
Of our fierce doings?
       Spare us yet awhile,
Father and God! O! spare us yet awhile!
Oh! let not English women drag their flight
Fainting beneath the burthen of their babes,
Of the sweet infants, that but yesterday
Laughed at the breast! Sons, brothers, husbands, all

Who ever gazed with fondness on the forms
Which grew up with you round the same fireside,
And all who ever heard the sabbath-bells
Without the infidel's scorn, make yourselves pure!
Stand forth! be men! repel an impious foe,
Impious and false, a light yet cruel race,
Who laugh away all virtue, mingling mirth
With deeds of murder; and still promising
Freedom, themselves too sensual to be free,
Poison life's amities, and cheat the heart
Of faith and quiet hope, and all that soothes,
And all that lifts the spirit! Stand we forth;
Render them back upon the insulted ocean,
And let them toss as idly on its waves
As the vile seaweed, which some mountain-blast
Swept from our shores! And oh! may we return
Not with a drunken triumph, but with fear,
Repenting of the wrongs with which we stung
So fierce a foe to frenzy!
      I have told,
O Britons! O my brethren! I have told
Most bitter truth, but without bitterness.
Nor deem my zeal or factious or mistimed;

For never can true courage dwell with them,
Who, playing tricks with conscience, dare not look
At their own vices. We have been too long
Dupes of a deep delusion! Some, belike,
Groaning with restless enmity, expect
All change from change of constituted power;
As if a Government had been a robe,
On which our vice and wretchedness were tagged
Like fancy-points and fringes, with the robe
Pulled off at pleasure. Fondly these attach
A radical causation to a few
Poor drudges of chastising Providence,
Who borrow all their hues and qualities
From our own folly and rank wickedness,
Which gave them birth and nursed them. Others,
  meanwhile,
Dote with a mad idolatry; and all
Who will not fall before their images,
And yield them worship, they are enemies
Even of their country!
        Such have I been deemed –
But, O dear Britain! O my Mother Isle!
Needs must thou prove a name most dear and holy

To me, a son, a brother, and a friend,
A husband, and a father! who revere
All bonds of natural love, and find them all
Within the limits of thy rocky shores.
O native Britain ! O my Mother Isle !
How shouldst thou prove aught else but dear and holy
To me, who from thy lakes and mountain-hills,
Thy clouds, thy quiet dales, thy rocks and seas,
Have drunk in all my intellectual life,
All sweet sensations, all ennobling thoughts,
All adoration of God in nature,
All lovely and all honourable things,
Whatever makes this mortal spirit feel
The joy and greatness of its future being?
There lives nor form nor feeling in my soul
Unborrowed from my country! O divine
And beauteous island! thou hast been my sole
And most magnificent temple, in the which
I walk with awe, and sing my stately songs,
Loving the God that made me! –
      May my fears,
My filial fears, be vain! and may the vaunts
And menace of the vengeful enemy

Pass like the gust, that roared and died away
In the distant tree: which heard, and only heard
In this low dell, bowed not the delicate grass.
      But now the gentle dew-fall sends abroad
The fruit-like perfume of the golden furze:
The light has left the summit of the hill,
Though still a sunny gleam lies beautiful,
Aslant the ivied beacon. Now farewell,
Farewell, awhile, O soft and silent spot!
On the green sheep-track, up the heathy hill,
Homeward I wind my way; and lo! recalled
From bodings that have well-nigh wearied me,
I find myself upon the brow, and pause
Startled! And after lonely sojourning
In such a quiet and surrounded nook,
This burst of prospect, here the shadowy main,
Dim tinted, there the mighty majesty
Of that huge amphitheatre of rich
And elmy fields, seems like society –
Conversing with the mind, and giving it
A livelier impulse and a dance of thought!
And now, belovéd Stowey! I behold
Thy church-tower, and, methinks, the four huge elms

Clustering, which mark the mansion of my friend;
And close behind them, hidden from my view,
Is my own lowly cottage, where my babe
And my babe's mother dwell in peace! With light
And quickened footsteps thitherward I tend,
Remembering thee, O green and silent dell!
And grateful, that by nature's quietness
And solitary musings, all my heart
Is softened, and made worthy to indulge
Love, and the thoughts that yearn for humankind.

Samuel Taylor Coleridge

* * *

THE PORTENT

Hanging from the beam,
    Slowly swaying (such the law),
Gaunt the shadow on your green,
    Shenandoah!
The cut is on the crown
    (Lo, John Brown),
And the stabs shall heal no more.

Hidden in the cap
    Is the anguish none can draw;
So your future veils its face,
    Shenandoah!
But the streaming beard is shown
    (Weird John Brown),
The meteor of the war.

Herman Melville

* * *

A WORD FOR THE HOUR

The firmament breaks up. In black eclipse
Light after light goes out. One evil star,
Luridly glaring through the smoke of war,
As in the dream of the Apocalypse,
Drags others down. Let us not weakly weep
Nor rashly threaten. Give us grace to keep
Our faith and patience; wherefore should we leap
On one hand into fratricidal fight,
Or, on the other, yield eternal right,
Frame lies of laws, and good and ill confound?

What fear we? Safe on freedom's vantage ground
Our feet are planted; let us there remain
In unrevengeful calm, no means untried
Which truth can sanction, no just claim denied,
The sad spectators of a suicide!
They break the lines of Union: shall we light
The fires of hell to weld anew the chain
On that red anvil where each blow is pain?
Draw we not even now a freer breath,
As from our shoulders falls a load of death
Loathsome as that the Tuscan's victim bore
When keen with life to a dead horror bound?
Why take we up the accursed thing again?
Pity, forgive, but urge them back no more
Who, drunk with passion, flaunt disunion's rag
With its vile reptile blazon. Let us press
The golden cluster on our brave old flag
In closer union, and, if numbering less,
Brighter shall shine the stars which still remain.

John Greenleaf Whittier

BEAT! BEAT! DRUMS!

I

Beat! beat! drums! – Blow! bugles! blow!

Through the windows – through doors – burst like a ruthless
force,

Into the solemn church, and scatter the congregation;

Into the school where the scholar is studying;

Leave not the bridegroom quiet – no happiness must he have
now with his bride;

Nor the peaceful farmer any peace, plowing his field or
gathering his grain;

So fierce you whirr and pound, you drums – so shrill you
bugles blow.

II

Beat! beat! drums! – Blow! bugles! blow!

Over the traffic of cities – over the rumble of wheels in the
streets:

Are beds prepared for sleepers at night in the houses? No
sleepers must sleep in those beds;

No bargainers' bargains by day – no brokers or speculators –
  Would they continue?
Would the talkers be talking? Would the singer attempt to sing?
Would the lawyer rise in the court to state his case before the
  judge?
Then rattle quicker, heavier drums – you bugles, wilder blow.

III

Beat! beat! drums! – Blow! bugles! blow!
Make no parley – stop for no expostulation;
Mind not the timid – mind not the weeper or prayer;
Mind not the old man beseeching the young man;
Let not the child's voice be heard, nor the mother's
  entreaties;
Make even the trestles to shake the dead, where they lie
  awaiting the hearses,
So strong you thump, O terrible drums – so loud you bugles
  blow.

Walt Whitman

EMBARCATION

(Southampton Docks: October 1899)

Here, where Vespasian's legions struck the sands,
And Cendric with the Saxons entered in,
And Henry's army leapt afloat to win
Convincing triumphs over neighbouring lands,

Vaster battalions press for further strands,
To argue in the selfsame bloody mode
Which this late age of thought, and pact, and code,
Still fails to mend. – Now deckward tramp the bands,

Yellow as autumn leaves, alive as spring;
And as each host draws out upon the sea
Beyond which lies the tragical To-be,
None dubious of the cause, none murmuring,

Wives, sisters, parents, wave white hands and smile,
As if they knew not that they weep the while.

Thomas Hardy

THE DYKES

We have no heart for the fishing, we have no hand for the oar –
All that our fathers taught us of old pleases us now no more.
All that our own hearts bid us believe we doubt where we do
not deny –
There is no proof in the bread we eat or rest in the toil we ply.

Look you, our foreshore stretches far through sea-gate, dyke,
and groin –
Made land all, that our fathers made, where the flats and the
fairway join.
They forced the sea a sea-league back. They died, and their
work stood fast.
We were born to peace in the lee of the dykes, but the time of
our peace is past.

Far off, the full tide clambers and slips, mouthing and testing
all,
Nipping the flanks of the water-gates, baying along the wall;
Turning the shingle, returning the shingle, changing the set of
the sand . . .
We are too far from the beach, men say, to know how the
outworks stand.

So we come down, uneasy, to look, uneasily pacing the beach.

These are the dykes our fathers made: we have never known a
breach.

Time and again has the gale blown by and we were not afraid;

Now we come only to look at the dykes – at the dykes our
fathers made.

O'er the marsh where the homesteads cower apart the harried
sunlight flies,

Shifts and considers, wanes and recovers, scatters and sickens
and dies –

An evil ember bedded in ash – a spark blown west by the
wind...

We are surrendered to night and the sea – the gale and the tide
behind!

At the bridge of the lower saltings the cattle gather and blare,

Roused by the feet of running men, dazed by the lantern
glare.

Unbar and let them away for their lives – the levels drown as
they stand,

Where the flood-wash forces the sluices aback and the ditches
deliver inland.

Ninefold deep to the top of the dykes the galloping breakers
    stride,
And their overcarried spray is a sea – a sea on the landward
    side.
Coming, like stallions they paw with their hooves, going they
    snatch with their teeth,
Till the bents and the furze and the sand are dragged out, and
    the old-time hurdles beneath.

Bid men gather fuel for fire, the tar, the oil and the tow –
Flame we shall need, not smoke, in the dark if the riddled
    seabanks go.
Bid the ringers watch in the tower (who knows how the dawn
    shall prove?)
Each with his rope between his feet and the trembling bells
    above.

Now we can only wait till the day, wait and apportion
    our shame.
These are the dykes our fathers left, but we would not look to
    the same.
Time and again were we warned of the dykes, time and again
    we delayed:

Now, it may fall, we have slain our sons, as our fathers we
have betrayed.

Walking along the wreck of the dykes, watching the work of
the seas!
These were the dykes our fathers made to our great profit
and ease.
But the peace is gone and the profit is gone, with the old sure
days withdrawn...
That our own houses show as strange when we come back in
the dawn!

Rudyard Kipling

* * *

ON THE DANGER OF WAR

Avert, High Wisdom, never vainly wooed,
This threat of War, that shows a land brain-sick.
When nations gain the pitch where rhetoric
Seems reason they are ripe for cannon's food.
Dark looms the issue though the cause be good,
But with the doubt 'tis our old devil's trick.

O now the down-slope of the lunatic
Illumine lest we redden of that brood.
For not since man in his first view of thee
Ascended to the heavens giving sign
Within him of deep sky and sounded sea,
Did he unforfeiting thy laws transgress;
In peril of his blood his ears incline
To drums whose loudness is their emptiness.

George Meredith

* * *

ON RECEIVING NEWS OF THE WAR

Snow is a strange white word.
No ice or frost
Has asked of bud or bird
For Winter's cost.

Yet ice and frost and snow
From earth to sky
This Summer land doth know.
No man knows why.

In all men's hearts it is.
Some spirit old
Hath turned with malign kiss
Our lives to mould.

Red fangs have torn His face.
God's blood is shed.
He mourns from His lone place
His children dead.

O! ancient crimson curse!
Corrode, consume.
Give back this universe
Its pristine bloom.

Isaac Rosenberg

* * *

MEN WHO MARCH AWAY

(Song of the Soldiers)

What of the faith and fire within us
Men who march away
Ere the barn-cocks say

Night is growing gray,
Leaving all here can win us;
What of the faith and fire within us
        Men who march away!

Is it a purblind prank, O think you,
        Friend with the musing eye,
        Who watch us stepping by,
        With doubt and dolorous sigh?
Can much pondering so hoodwink you?
Is it a purblind prank, O think you,
        Friend with the musing eye?

Nay. We see well what we are doing,
        Though some may not see –
        Dalliers as they be –
        England's need are we;
Her distress would leave us rueing:
Nay. We well see what we are doing,
        Though some may not see!

In our heart of hearts believing
        Victory crowns the just,
        And that braggarts must

Surely bite the dust,
Press we to the field ungrieving,
In our heart of hearts believing
Victory crowns the just.

Hence the faith and fire within us
Men who march away
Ere the barn-cocks say
Night is growing gray,
Leaving all that here can win us;
Hence the faith and fire within us
Men who march away.

Thomas Hardy

* * *

THE GREAT LOVER

I have been so great a lover: filled my days
So proudly with the splendour of Love's praise,
The pain, the calm, and the astonishment,
Desire illimitable, and still content,
And all dear names men use, to cheat despair,
For the perplexed and viewless streams that bear

Our hearts at random down the dark of life.
Now, ere the unthinking silence on that strife
Steals down, I would cheat drowsy Death so far,
My night shall be remembered for a star
That outshone all the suns of all men's days.
Shall I not crown them with immortal praise
Whom I have loved, who have given me, dared with me
High secrets, and in darkness knelt to see
The inenarrable godhead of delight?
Love is a flame; we have beaconed the world's night.
A city: and we have built it, these and I.
An emperor: we have taught the world to die.
So, for their sakes I loved, ere I go hence,
And the high cause of Love's magnificence,
And to keep loyalties young, I'll write those names
Golden for ever, eagles, crying flames,
And set them as a banner, that men may know,
To dare the generations, burn, and blow
Out on the wind of Time, shining and streaming...
These I have loved:

       White plates and cups, clean-gleaming,
Ringed with blue lines; and feathery, faery dust;
Wet roofs, beneath the lamp-light; the strong crust
Of friendly bread; and many-tasting food;

Rainbows; and the blue bitter smoke of wood;
And radiant raindrops couching in cool flowers;
And flowers themselves, that sway through sunny hours,
Dreaming of moths that drink them under the moon;
Then, the cool kindliness of sheets, that soon
Smooth away trouble; and the rough male kiss
Of blankets; grainy wood; live hair that is
Shining and free; blue-massing clouds; the keen
Unpassioned beauty of a great machine;
The benison of hot water; furs to touch;
The good smell of old clothes; and other such –
The comfortable smell of friendly fingers,
Hair's fragrance, and the musty reek that lingers
About dead leaves and last year's ferns . . .

      Dear names,
And thousand others throng to me! Royal flames;
Sweet water's dimpling laugh from tap or spring;
Holes in the ground; and voices that do sing:
Voices in laughter, too; and body's pain,
Soon turned to peace; and the deep-panting train;
Firm sands; the little dulling edge of foam
That browns and dwindles as the wave goes home;
And washen stones, gay for an hour; the cold
Graveness of iron; moist black earthen mould;

Sleep; and high places; footprints in the dew;
And oaks; and brown horse-chestnuts, glossy-new;
And new-peeled sticks; and shining pools on grass; –
All these have been my loves. And these shall pass.
Whatever passes not, in the great hour,
Nor all my passion, all my prayers, have power
To hold them with me through the gate of Death.
They'll play deserter, turn with the traitor breath,
Break the high bond we made, and sell Love's trust
And sacramented covenant to the dust.
 – Oh, never a doubt but, somewhere, I shall wake,
And give what's left of love again, and make
New friends, now strangers . . .

      But the best I've known,
Stays here, and changes, breaks, grows old, is blown
About the winds of the world, and fades from brains
Of living men, and dies.

      Nothing remains.

O dear my loves, O faithless, once again
This one last gift I give: that after men
Shall know, and later lovers, far removed
Praise you, 'All these were lovely'; say, 'He loved.'

Rupert Brooke

Lines Before Going

Soon is the night of our faring to regions unknown,
There not to flinch at the challenge suddenly thrown
By the great process of Being – daily to see
The utmost that life has of horror and yet to be
Calm and the masters of fear. Aware that the soul
Lives as a part and alone for the weal of the whole,
So shall the mind be free from the pain of regret,
Vain and enfeebling, firm in each venture, and yet
Brave not as those who despair, but keen to maintain,
Though not assured, hope in beneficent pain.
Hope that the truth of the world is not what appears,
Hope in the triumph of man for the price of his tears.

Alexander Robertson

* * *

The Send-Off

Down the close, darkening lanes they sang their way
To the siding-shed,
And lined the train with faces grimly gay.

Their breasts were stuck all white with wreath and spray
As men's are, dead.

Dull porters watched them, and a casual tramp
Stood staring hard,
Sorry to miss them from the upland camp.
Then, unmoved, signals nodded, and a lamp
Winked to the guard.

So secretly, like wrongs hushed-up, they went.
They were not ours:
We never heard to which front these were sent.
Nor there if they yet mock what women meant
Who gave them flowers.
Shall they return to beatings of great bells
In wild trainloads?
A few, a few, too few for drums and yells,
May creep back, silent, to still village wells
Up half-known roads.

Wilfred Owen

ALL DAY IT HAS RAINED

All day it has rained, and we on the edge of the moors
Have sprawled in our bell-tents, moody and dull as boors,
Groundsheets and blankets spread on the muddy ground
And from the first grey wakening we have found
No refuge from the skirmishing fine rain
And the wind that made the canvas heave and flap
And the taut wet guy-ropes ravel out and snap,
All day the rain has glided, wave and mist and dream,
Drenching the gorse and heather, a gossamer stream
Too light to stir the acorns that suddenly
Snatched from their cups by the wild south-westerly
Pattered against the tent and our upturned dreaming faces.
And we stretched out, unbuttoning our braces,
Smoking a Woodbine, darning dirty socks,
Reading the Sunday papers – I saw a fox
And mentioned it in the note I scribbled home;
And we talked of girls and dropping bombs on Rome,
And thought of the quiet dead and the loud celebrities
Exhorting us to slaughter, and the herded refugees;
 – Yet thought softly, morosely of them, and as indifferently
As of ourselves or those whom we
For years have loved, and will again

Tomorrow maybe love; but now it is the rain
Possesses us entirely, the twilight and the rain.
And I can remember nothing dearer or more to my heart
Than the children I watched in the woods on Saturday
Shaking down burning chestnuts for the schoolyard's merry play
Or the shaggy patient dog who followed me
By Sheet and Steep and up the wooded scree
To the Shoulder o' Mutton where Edward Thomas brooded long
On death and beauty – till a bullet stopped his song.

Alun Lewis

BROTHERS IN ARMS

We husband the ancient glory
In these bared necks and hands.
Not broke is the forge of Mars;
But a subtler brain beats iron
To shoe the hoofs of death…

THE REVENGE

I

At Flores, in the Azores, Sir Richard Grenville lay,

And a pinnace, like a flutter'd bird, came flying from far away;

'Spanish ships of war at sea! we have sighted fifty-three!'

Then sware Lord Thomas Howard: ''Fore God I am no coward;

But I cannot meet them here, for my ships are out of gear,

And the half my men are sick. I must fly, but follow quick.

We are six ships of the line; can we fight with fifty-three?'

II

Then spake Sir Richard Grenville: 'I know you are no coward;

You fly them for a moment to fight with them again.

But I've ninety men and more that are lying sick ashore.

I should count myself the coward if I left them, my Lord
   Howard,

To these Inquisition dogs and the devildoms of Spain.'

III

So Lord Howard past away with five ships of war that day,

Till he melted like a cloud in the silent summer heaven;

But Sir Richard bore in hand all his sick men from the land

Very carefully and slow,

Men of Bideford in Devon,

And we laid them on the ballast down below:

For we brought them all aboard,

And they blest him in their pain, that they were not left to
    Spain,

To the thumbscrew and the stake, for the glory of the Lord.

IV

He had only a hundred seamen to work the ship and to fight,

And he sailed away from Flores till the Spaniard came in sight,

With his huge sea-castles heaving upon the weather bow.

'Shall we fight or shall we fly?

Good Sir Richard, tell us now,

For to fight is but to die!

There'll be little of us left by the time this sun be set.'

And Sir Richard said again: 'We be all good Englishmen.

Let us bang these dogs of Seville, the children of the devil,

For I never turn'd my back upon Don or devil yet.'

V

Sir Richard spoke and he laugh'd, and we roar'd a hurrah and so

The little Revenge ran on sheer into the heart of the foe,

With her hundred fighters on deck, and her ninety sick below;

For half of their fleet to the right and half to the left were seen,
And the little Revenge ran on thro' the long sea-lane between.

VI

Thousands of their soldiers look'd down from their decks and
    laugh'd,
Thousands of their seamen made mock at the mad little craft
Running on and on, till delay'd
By their mountain-like San Philip that, of fifteen hundred tons,
And up-shadowing high above us with her yawning tiers of
    guns,
Took the breath from our sails, and we stay'd.

VII

And while now the great San Philip hung above us like a
    cloud
Whence the thunderbolt will fall
Long and loud,
Four galleons drew away
From the Spanish fleet that day.
And two upon the larboard and two upon the starboard lay,
And the battle-thunder broke from them all.

VIII

But anon the great San Philip, she bethought herself and went,
Having that within her womb that had left her ill content;
And the rest they came aboard us, and they fought us hand to
  hand,
For a dozen times they came with their pikes and musqueteers,
And a dozen times we shook 'em off as a dog that shakes his
  ears
When he leaps from the water to the land.

IX

And the sun went down, and the stars came out far over the
  summer sea,
But never a moment ceased the fight of the one and the fifty-
  three.
Ship after ship, the whole night long, their high-built galleons
  came,
Ship after ship, the whole night long, with her battle-thunder
  and flame;
Ship after ship, the whole night long, drew back with her dead
  and her shame.
For some were sunk and many were shatter'd and so could
  fight us no more –

God of battles, was ever a battle like this in the world
    before?

X

For he said, 'Fight on! fight on!'
Tho' his vessel was all but a wreck;
And it chanced that, when half of the short summer night was
    gone,
With a grisly wound to be drest he had left the deck,
But a bullet struck him that was dressing it suddenly dead,
And himself he was wounded again in the side and the head,
And he said, 'Fight on! fight on!'

XI

And the night went down, and the sun smiled out far over the
    summer sea,
And the Spanish fleet with broken sides lay round us all in a
    ring;
But they dared not touch us again, for they fear'd that we still
    could sting,
So they watch'd what the end would be.
And we had not fought them in vain,
But in perilous plight were we,

Seeing forty of our poor hundred were slain,

And half of the rest of us maim'd for life

In the crash of the cannonades and the desperate strife;

And the sick men down in the hold were most of them stark
and cold,

And the pikes were all broken or bent, and the powder was all
of it spent;

And the masts and the rigging were lying over the side;

But Sir Richard cried in his English pride:

'We have fought such a fight for a day and a night

As may never be fought again!

We have won great glory, my men!

And a day less or more

At sea or ashore,

We die – does it matter when?

Sink me the ship, Master Gunner – sink her, split her in twain!

Fall into the hands of God, not into the hands of Spain!'

XII

And the gunner said, 'Ay, ay,' but the seamen made reply:

'We have children, we have wives,

And the Lord hath spared our lives.

We will make the Spaniard promise, if we yield, to let us go;

We shall live to fight again and to strike another blow.'
And the lion there lay dying, and they yielded to the foe.

XIII

And the stately Spanish men to their flagship bore him then,
Where they laid him by the mast, old Sir Richard caught at last,
And they praised him to his face with their courtly foreign
    grace;
But he rose upon their decks, and he cried:
'I have fought for Queen and Faith like a valiant man and true;
I have only done my duty as a man is bound to do.
With a joyful spirit I Sir Richard Grenville die!'
And he fell upon their decks, and he died.

XIV

And they stared at the dead that had been so valiant and true,
And had holden the power and glory of Spain so cheap
That he dared her with one little ship and his English few;
Was he devil or man? He was devil for aught they knew,
But they sank his body with honor down into the deep.
And they mann'd the Revenge with a swarthier alien crew,
And away she sail'd with her loss and long'd for her own;
When a wind from the lands they had ruin'd awoke from sleep,

And the water began to heave and the weather to moan,
And or ever that evening ended a great gale blew,
And a wave like the wave that is raised by an earthquake grew,
Till it smote on their hulls and their sails and their masts and
     their flags,
And the whole sea plunged and fell on the shot-shatter'd navy
     of Spain,
And the little Revenge herself went down by the island crags
To be lost evermore in the main.

Alfred, Lord Tennyson

* * *

INCIDENT OF THE FRENCH CAMP

You know, we French storm'd Ratisbon:
     A mile or so away
On a little mound, Napoleon
     Stood on our storming-day;
With neck out-thrust, you fancy how,
     Legs wide, arms locked behind,
As if to balance the prone brow
     Oppressive with its mind.

Just as perhaps he mus'd 'My plans
      That soar, to earth may fall,
Let once my army leader Lannes
      Waver at yonder wall' –
Out 'twixt the battery smokes there flew
      A rider, bound on bound
Full-galloping; nor bridle drew
      Until he reach'd the mound.

Then off there flung in smiling joy,
      And held himself erect
By just his horse's mane, a boy:
      You hardly could suspect –
(So tight he kept his lips compress'd,
      Scarce any blood came through)
You look'd twice ere you saw his breast
      Was all but shot in two.

'Well,' cried he, 'Emperor, by God's grace
      We've got you Ratisbon!
The Marshal's in the market-place,
      And you'll be there anon
To see your flag-bird flap his vans

Where I, to heart's desire,
Perch'd him!' The chief's eye flash'd; his plans
Soared up again like fire.

The chief's eye flashed; but presently
Softened itself, as sheathes
A film the mother-eagle's eye
When her bruis'd eaglet breathes;
'You're wounded!' 'Nay,' the soldier's pride
Touched to the quick, he said:
'I'm killed, Sire!' And his chief beside,
Smiling the boy fell dead.

Robert Browning

* * *

CAVALRY CROSSING A FORD

A line in long array, where they wind betwixt green islands;
They take a serpentine course – their arms flash in the sun –
    Hark to the musical clank;
Behold the silvery river – in it the splashing horses, loitering,
    stop to drink;
Behold the brown-faced men – each group, each person, a
    picture – the negligent rest on the saddles;

Some emerge on the opposite bank – others are just entering
   the ford – while,
Scarlet, and blue, and snowy white,
The guidon flags flutter gaily in the wind.

Walt Whitman

* * *

Vigil Strange I Kept on the Field

Vigil strange I kept on the field one night:
When you, my son and my comrade, dropt at my side that day,
One look I but gave, which your dear eyes return'd, with a
   look I shall never forget;
One touch of your hand to mine, O boy, reach'd up as you lay
   on the ground;
Then onward I sped in the battle, the even-contested battle;
Till late in the night reliev'd, to the place at last again I made
   my way;
Found you in death so cold, dear comrade – found your body,
   son of responding kisses, (never again on earth responding);
Bared your face in the starlight – curious the scene – cool blew
   the moderate night-wind;

Long there and then in vigil I stood, dimly around me the
battlefield spreading;

Vigil wondrous and vigil sweet, there in the fragrant silent
night;

But not a tear fell, not even a long-drawn sigh – long, long I
gazed;

Then on the earth partially reclining, sat by your side, leaning
my chin in my hands;

Passing sweet hours, immortal and mystic hours with you,
dearest comrade – not a tear, not a word;

Vigil of silence, love and death – vigil for you my son and my
soldier,

As onward silently stars aloft, eastward new ones upward
stole;

Vigil final for you, brave boy, (I could not save you, swift was
your death,

I faithfully loved you and cared for you living – I think we
shall surely meet again);

Till at latest lingering of the night, indeed just as the dawn
appear'd,

My comrade I wrapt in his blanket, envelop'd well his form,

Folded the blanket well, tucking it carefully over head, and
carefully under feet;

And there and then, and bathed by the rising sun, my son in
his grave, in his rude-dug grave I deposited;
Ending my vigil strange with that – vigil of night and
battlefield dim;
Vigil for boy of responding kisses, (never again on earth
responding);
Vigil for comrade swiftly slain – vigil I never forget, how as
day brighten'd,
I rose from the chill ground, and folded my soldier well in his
blanket,
And buried him where he fell.

Walt Whitman

* * *

ARITHMETIC ON THE FRONTIER

A great and glorious thing it is
    To learn, for seven years or so,
The Lord knows what of that and this,
    Ere reckoned fit to face the foe –
The flying bullet down the Pass,
That whistles clear: 'All flesh is grass.'

Three hundred pounds per annum spent
> On making brain and body meeter
For all the murderous intent
> Comprised in 'villanous saltpetre!'
And after – ask the Yusufzaies
What comes of all our 'ologies.

A scrimmage in a Border Station –
> A canter down some dark defile –
Two thousand pounds of education
> Drops to a ten-rupee jezail –
The Crammer's boast, the Squadron's pride,
Shot like a rabbit in a ride!

No proposition Euclid wrote,
> No formulae the textbooks know,
Will turn the bullet from your coat,
> Or ward the tulwar's downward blow
Strike hard who cares – shoot straight who can –
The odds are on the cheaper man.

One sword-knot stolen from the camp
> Will pay for all the school expenses

Of any Kurrum Valley scamp
      Who knows no word of moods and tenses,
But, being blessed with perfect sight,
Picks off our messmates left and right.

With home-bred hordes the hillsides teem,
      The troop-ships bring us one by one,
At vast expense of time and steam,
      To slay Afridis where they run.
The 'captives of our bow and spear'
Are cheap – alas! as we are dear.

Rudyard Kipling

* * *

THE COLONEL'S SOLILOQUY

(Southampton Docks: October, 1899)

'The quay recedes. Hurrah! Ahead we go! . . .
It's true I've been accustomed now to home,
And joints get rusty, and one's limbs may grow
      More fit to rest than roam.

'But I can stand as yet fair stress and strain;
There's not a little steel beneath the rust;
My years mount somewhat, but here's to 't again!
       And if I fall, I must.

'God knows that for myself I've scanty care;
Past scrimmages have proved as much to all;
In Eastern lands and South I've had my share
       Both of the blade and ball.

'And where those villains ripped me in the flitch
With their old iron in my early time,
I'm apt at change of wind to feel a twitch,
       Or at a change of clime.

'And what my mirror shows me in the morning
Has more of blotch and wrinkle than of bloom;
My eyes, too, heretofore all glasses scorning,
       Have just a touch of rheum...

'Now sounds "The Girl I've left behind me" – Ah,
The years, the ardours, wakened by that tune!

Time was when, with the crowd's farewell "Hurrah!"
    'Twould lift me to the moon.

'But now it's late to leave behind me one
Who if, poor soul, her man goes underground,
Will not recover as she might have done
    In days when hopes abound.

'She's waving from the wharfside, palely grieving,
As down we draw… Her tears make little show,
Yet now she suffers more than at my leaving
    Some twenty years ago.

'I pray those left at home will care for her!
I shall come back; I have before; though when
The Girl you leave behind you is a grandmother,
    Things may not be as then.'

Thomas Hardy

BRIDGE-GUARD IN THE KARROO

'and will supply details to guard the Blood River Bridge.' –
District Orders: Lines of Communication, South African War.

Sudden the desert changes,
  The raw glare softens and clings,
Till the aching Oudtshoorn ranges
  Stand up like the thrones of kings –

Ramparts of slaughter and peril –
  Blazing, amazing, aglow –
'Twixt the skyline's belting beryl
  And the wine-dark flats below.

Royal the pageant closes,
  Lit by the last of the sun –
Opal and ash-of-roses,
  Cinnamon, umber, and dun.

The twilight swallows the thicket,
  The starlight reveals the ridge;
The whistle shrills to the picket –
  We are changing guard on the bridge.

(Few, forgotten and lonely,
   Where the empty metals shine –
No, not combatants – only
   Details guarding the line.)

We slip through the broken panel
   Of fence by the ganger's shed;
We drop to the waterless channel
   And the lean track overhead;

We stumble on refuse of rations,
   The beef and the biscuit-tins;
We take our appointed stations,
   And the endless night begins.

We hear the Hottentot herders
   As the sheep click past to the fold –
And the click of the restless girders
   As the steel contracts in the cold –

Voices of jackals calling
   And, loud in the hush between,

A morsel of dry earth falling
    From the flanks of the scarred ravine.

And the solemn firmament marches,
    And the hosts of heaven rise
Framed through the iron arches –
    Banded and barred by the ties,

Till we feel the far track humming,
    And we see her headlight plain,
And we gather and wait her coming –
    The wonderful northbound train.

(Few, forgotten and lonely,
    Where the white car-windows shine –
No, not combatants – only
    Details guarding the line.)

Quick, ere the gift escape us!
    Out of the darkness we reach
For a handful of week-old papers
    And a mouthful of human speech.

And the monstrous heaven rejoices,
And the earth allows again,
Meetings, greetings, and voices
Of women talking with men.

So we return to our places,
As out on the bridge she rolls;
And the darkness covers our faces,
And the darkness re-enters our souls.

More than a little lonely
Where the lessening tail-lights shine.
No – not combatants – only
Details guarding the line!

Rudyard Kipling

* * *

MARCHING (AS SEEN FROM THE LEFT FILE)

My eyes catch ruddy necks
Sturdily pressed back –
All a red brick moving glint.

Like flaming pendulums, hands
Swing across the khaki –
Mustard-coloured khaki –
To the automatic feet.

We husband the ancient glory
In these bared necks and hands.
Not broke is the forge of Mars;
But a subtler brain beats iron
To shoe the hoofs of death,
(Who paws dynamic air now).
Blind fingers loose an iron cloud
To rain immortal darkness
On strong eyes.

Isaac Rosenberg

* * *

I TRACKED A DEAD MAN DOWN A TRENCH

I tracked a dead man down a trench,
I knew not he was dead.
They told me he had gone that way,
And there his foot-marks led.

The trench was long and close and curved,
It seemed without an end;
And as I threaded each new bay
I thought to see my friend.

I went there stooping to the ground.
For, should I raise my head,
Death watched to spring; and how should
A dead man find the dead?

At last I saw his back. He crouched
As still as still could be,
And when I called his name aloud
He did not answer me.

The floor-way of the trench was wet
Where he was crouching dead:
The water of the pool was brown,
And round him it was red.

I stole up softly where he stayed
With head hung down all slack,
And on his shoulders laid my hands
And drew him gently back.

And then, as I had guessed, I saw
His head, and how the crown –
I saw then why he crouched so still,
And why his head hung down.

W. S. S. Lyon

* * *

FUTILITY

Move him into the sun –
Gently its touch awoke him once,
At home, whispering of fields unsown.
Always it woke him, even in France,
Until this morning and this snow.
If anything might rouse him now
The kind old sun will know.

Think how it wakes the seeds –
Woke, once, the clays of a cold star.
Are limbs, so dear-achieved, are sides,
Full-nerved – still warm – too hard to stir?
Was it for this the clay grew tall?

– O what made fatuous sunbeams toil
To break earth's sleep at all?

Wilfred Owen

* * *

LOUSE HUNTING

Nudes – stark and glistening,
Yelling in lurid glee. Grinning faces
And raging limbs
Whirl over the floor on fire.
For a shirt verminously busy
Yon soldier tore from his throat, with oaths
Godhead might shrink at, but not the lice.
And soon the shirt was aflare
Over the candle he'd lit while we lay.

Then we all sprang up and stript
To hunt the verminous brood.
Soon like a demon's pantomime
The place was raging.
See the silhouettes agape,

See the glibbering shadows
Mixed with the battled arms on the wall.
See gargantuan hooked fingers
Pluck in supreme flesh
To smutch supreme littleness.
See the merry limbs in hot Highland fling
Because some wizard vermin
Charmed from the quiet this revel
When our ears were half lulled
By the dark music
Blown from Sleep's trumpet.

Isaac Rosenberg

* * *

DISABLED

He sat in a wheeled chair, waiting for dark,
And shivered in his ghastly suit of grey,
Legless, sewn short at elbow. Through the park
Voices of boys rang saddening like a hymn,
Voices of play and pleasure after day,
Till gathering sleep had mothered them from him.
About this time Town used to swing so gay

When glow-lamps budded in the light blue trees,
And girls glanced lovelier as the air grew dim,
– In the old times, before he threw away his knees.
Now he will never feel again how slim
Girls' waists are, or how warm their subtle hands,
All of them touch him like some queer disease.

There was an artist silly for his face,
For it was younger than his youth, last year.
Now, he is old; his back will never brace;
He's lost his colour very far from here,
Poured it down shell-holes till the veins ran dry,
And half his lifetime lapsed in the hot race
And leap of purple spurted from his thigh.

One time he liked a bloodsmear down his leg,
After the matches, carried shoulder-high.
It was after football, when he'd drunk a peg,
He thought he'd better join. – He wonders why.
Someone had said he'd look a god in kilts,
That's why; and maybe, too, to please his Meg,
Aye, that was it, to please the giddy jilts
He asked to join. He didn't have to beg;
Smiling they wrote his lie: aged nineteen years.

Germans he scarcely thought of; all their guilt
And Austria's, did not move him. And no fears
Of Fear came yet. He thought of jewelled hilts
For daggers in plaid socks; of smart salutes;
And care of arms; and leave; and pay arrears;
Esprit de corps; and hints for young recruits.
And soon, he was drafted out with drums and cheers.

Some cheered him home, but not as crowds cheer Goal.
Only a solemn man who brought him fruits
Thanked him; and then enquired about his soul.

Now, he will spend a few sick years in institutes,
And do what things the rules consider wise,
And take whatever pity they may dole.
Tonight he noticed how the women's eyes
Passed from him to the strong men that were whole.
How cold and late it is! Why don't they come
And put him into bed? Why don't they come?

Wilfred Owen

Light After Darkness

Once more the Night, like some great dark drop-scene
Eclipsing horrors for a brief *entr'acte*,
Descends, lead-weighty. Now the space between,
Fringed with the eager eyes of men, is racked
By spark-tailed lights, curvetting far and high,
Swift smoke-flecked coursers, raking the black sky.

And as each sinks in ashes grey, one more
Rises to fall, and so through all the hours
They strive like petty empires by the score,
Each confident of its success and powers,
And, hovering at its zenith, each will show
Pale, rigid faces, lying dead, below.

There shall they lie, tainting the innocent air,
Until the dawn, deep veiled in mournful grey,
Sadly and quietly shall lay them bare,
The broken heralds of a doleful day.

E. Wyndham Tennant

THE KITCHENER CHAP

He wore twin stripes of gold upon
    An empty tunic sleeve;
His eyes were blue, his face so young
    One hardly could believe
That he had seen the death and hate
    That make the whole world grieve.

His hair was fair, his eyes were blue,
    I thought that I could see
(Just when his sunny smile came through)
    The lad he used to be:
Dear happy little mother's lad
    Of only two or three.

But when across his eyes there came
    A sudden look of pain –
His mouth set very hard and straight,
    He was a man again.
He gave his shattered dreams of youth
    That England might remain.

I felt hot tears rise to my eyes
    When I looked at the lad;

Brave, gallant, shattered, smiling youth –
    He gave us all he had;
For youth so fair, so sorely hurt
    All England's heart is sad.

He passed me on a crowded street,
    We did not meet again;
He showed me in a sudden flash
    Our England's pride and pain.
And when all is long forgot
    His memory shall remain.

Horace Bray

* * *

MENTAL CASES

Who are these? Why sit they here in twilight?
Wherefore rock they, purgatorial shadows,
Drooping tongues from jaws that slob their relish,
Baring teeth that leer like skulls' teeth wicked?
Stroke on stroke of pain – but what slow panic,
Gouged these chasms round their fretted sockets?
Ever from their hair and through their hands' palms

Misery swelters. Surely we have perished
Sleeping, and walk hell; but who these hellish?

– These are men whose minds the Dead have ravished.
Memory fingers in their hair of murders,
Multitudinous murders they once witnessed.
Wading sloughs of flesh these helpless wander,
Treading blood from lungs that had loved laughter.
Always they must see these things and hear them,
Batter of guns and shatter of flying muscles,
Carnage incomparable, and human squander
Rucked too thick for these men's extrication.

Therefore still their eyeballs shrink tormented
Back into their brains, because on their sense
Sunlight seems a bloodsmear; night comes blood-black;
Dawn breaks open like a wound that bleeds afresh.
– Thus their heads wear this hilarious, hideous,
Awful falseness of set-smiling corpses.
– Thus their hands are plucking at each other;
Picking at the rope-knouts of their scourging;
Snatching after us who smote them, brother,
Pawing us who dealt them war and madness.

Wilfred Owen

In Flanders Fields

In Flanders fields the poppies blow
Between the crosses, row on row,
 That mark our place; and in the sky
 The larks, still bravely singing, fly
Scarce heard amid the guns below.

We are the Dead. Short days ago
We lived, felt dawn, saw sunset glow,
 Loved and were loved, and now we lie
 In Flanders fields.

Take up our quarrel with the foe:
To you from failing hands we throw
 The torch; be yours to hold it high.
 If ye break faith with us who die
We shall not sleep, though poppies grow
 In Flanders fields.

John McCrae

THE HEAT OF BATTLE

Of them who running on that last high place

Leapt to swift unseen bullets, or went up

On the hot blast and fury of hell's upsurge,

Or plunged and fell away past this world's verge,

Some say God caught them even before they fell.

THE BATTLE OF BUNANBURH

I

Athelstan King,
> Lord among Earls,
> Bracelet-bestower and
> Baron of Barons,
> He with his brother,
> Edmund Atheling,
> Gaining a lifelong
> Glory in battle,
> Slew with the sword-edge
> There by Brunanburh,
> Brake the shield-wall,
> Hew'd the lindenwood,
> Hack'd the battleshield,

Sons of Edward with hammer'd brands.

II

> Theirs was a greatness
> Got from their Grandsires –
> Theirs that so often in
> Strife with their enemies

Struck for their hoards and their hearths and their homes.

III

Bow'd the spoiler,
Bent the Scotsman,
Fell the shipcrews
Doom'd to the death.
All the field with blood of the fighters
Flow'd, from when first the great
Sun-star of morningtide,
Lamp of the Lord God
Lord everlasting,
Glode over earth till the glorious creature
Sank to his setting.

IV

There lay many a man
Marr'd by the javelin,
Men of the Northland
Shot over shield.
There was the Scotsman
Weary of war.

V

We the West-Saxons,
Long as the daylight

Lasted, in companies
Troubled the track of the host that we hated,
Grimly with swords that were sharp from the grindstone,
Fiercely we hack'd at the flyers before us.

VI

Mighty the Mercian,
Hard was his hand-play,
Sparing not any of
Those that with Anlaf,
Warriors over the
Weltering waters
Borne in the bark's bosom,
Drew to this island:
Doom'd to the death.

VII

Five young kings put asleep by the sword-stroke,
Seven strong Earls of the army of Anlaf
Fell on the war-field, numberless numbers,
Shipmen and Scotsmen.

VIII

Then the Norse leader.
Dire was his need of it,
Few were his following,
Fled to his warship
Fleeted his vessel to sea with the king in it.
Saving his life on the fallow flood.

IX

Also the crafty one,
Constantinus,
Crept to his North again,
Hoar-headed hero!

X

Slender warrant had
He to be proud of
The welcome of war-knives –
He that was reft of his
Folk and his friends that had
Fallen in conflict,
Leaving his son too
Lost in the carnage,

Mangled to morsels,
A youngster in war!

XI

Slender reason had
He to be glad of
The clash of the war-glaive –
Traitor and trickster
And spurner of treaties –
He nor had Anlaf
With armies so broken
A reason for bragging
That they had the better
In perils of battle
On places of slaughter –
The struggle of standards,
The rush of the javelins,
The crash of the charges,
The wielding of weapons –
The play that they play'd with
The children of Edward.

XII

Then with their nail'd prows
Parted the Norsemen, a
Blood-redden'd relic of
Javelins over
The jarring breaker, the deep-sea billow,
Shaping their way toward Dyflen again,
Shamed in their souls.

XIII

Also the brethren,
King and Atheling,
Each in his glory,
Went to his own in his own West-Saxonland,
Glad of the war.

XIV

Many a carcase they left to be carrion,
Many a livid one, many a sallow-skin –
Left for the white-tail'd eagle to tear it, and
Left for the horny-nibb'd raven to rend it, and
Gave to the garbaging war-hawk to gorge it, and
That gray beast, the wolf of the weald.

XV

Never had huger
Slaughter of heroes
Slain by the sword-edge –
Such as old writers
Have writ of in histories –
Hapt in this isle, since
Up from the East hither
Saxon and Angle from
Over the broad billow
Broke into Britain with
Haughty war-workers who
Harried the Welshman, when
Earls that were lured by the
Hunger of glory gat
Hold of the land.

Alfred, Lord Tennyson

THE BATTLE OF NASEBY

Oh! wherefore come ye forth in triumph from the north,
With your hands, and your feet, and your raiment all red?
And wherefore doth your rout send forth a joyous shout?
And whence be the grapes of the wine-press that ye tread?

Oh! evil was the root, and bitter was the fruit,
And crimson was the juice of the vintage that we trod;
For we trampled on the throng of the haughty and the strong,
Who sate in the high places and slew the saints of God.

It was about the noon of a glorious day of June,
That we saw their banners dance and their cuirasses shine,
And the man of blood was there, with his long essenced hair,
And Astley, and Sir Marmaduke, and Rupert of the Rhine.

Like a servant of the Lord, with his Bible and his sword,
The general rode along us to form us for the fight;
When a murmuring sound broke out, and swelled into a shout
Among the godless horsemen upon the tyrant's right.

And hark! like the roar of the billows on the shore,
The cry of battle rises along their charging line:

For God! for the Cause! for the Church! for the laws!
For Charles, king of England, and Rupert of the Rhine!

The furious German comes, with his clarions and his drums,
His bravoes of Alsatia and pages of Whitehall;
They are bursting on our flanks! Grasp your pikes! Close your
    ranks!
For Rupert never comes, but to conquer or to fall.

They are here – they rush on – we are broken – we are gone –
Our left is borne before them like stubble on the blast.
O Lord, put forth thy might! O Lord, defend the right!
Stand back to back, in God's name! and fight it to the last!

Stout Skippen hath a wound – the centre hath given ground.
Hark! Hark! what means the trampling of horsemen on our
    rear?
Whose banner do I see, boys? 'Tis he! thank God! 'tis he, boys!
Bear up another minute! Brave Oliver is here!

Their heads all stooping low, their points all in a row:
Like a whirlwind on the trees, like a deluge on the dikes,
Our cuirassiers have burst on the ranks of the accurst,
And at a shock have scattered the forest of his pikes.

Fast, fast, the gallants ride, in some safe nook to hide
Their coward heads, predestined to rot on Temple Bar;
And he – he turns! he flies! shame on those cruel eyes
That bore to look on torture, and dare not look on war!

Ho, comrades! scour the plain; and ere ye strip the slain,
First give another stab to make your search secure;
Then shake from sleeves and pockets their broad-pieces and
    lockets,
The tokens of the wanton, the plunder of the poor.

Fools! your doublets shone with gold, and your hearts were
    gay and bold,
When you kissed your lily hands to your lemans today;
And tomorrow shall the fox from her chambers in the rocks
Lead forth her tawny cubs to howl above the prey.

Where be your tongues, that late mocked at heaven, and hell,
    and fate?
And the fingers that once were so busy with your blades?
Your perfumed satin clothes, your catches and your oaths?
Your stage plays and your sonnets, your diamonds and your
    spades?

Down! down! forever down, with the mitre and the crown!
With the Belial of the court, and the Mammon of the Pope!
There is woe in Oxford halls, there is wail in Durham's stalls;
The Jesuit smites his bosom, the bishop rends his cope.

And she of the seven hills shall mourn her children's ills,
And tremble when she thinks on the edge of England's sword;
And the kings of earth in fear shall shudder when they hear
What the hand of God hath wrought for the houses and the word.

Thomas Babington Macaulay

* * *

HOHENLINDEN

On Linden when the sun was low,
All bloodless lay the untrodden snow;
And dark as winter was the flow
　　Of Iser, rolling rapidly.

But Linden saw another sight,
When the drum beat, at dead of night
Commanding fires of death to light
　　The darkness of her scenery.

By torch and trumpet fast array'd
Each horseman drew his battle blade,
And furious every charger neigh'd,
　　To join the dreadful revelry.

Then shook the hills with thunder riven;
Then rushed the steed to battle driven;
And louder than the bolts of Heaven
　　Far flash'd the red artillery.

And redder yet those fires shall glow
On Linden's hills of stainéd snow;
And darker yet shall be the flow
　　Of Iser, rolling rapidly.

'Tis morn; but scarce yon revel sun
Can pierce the war-clouds, rolling dun,
Where furious Frank and fiery Hun
　　Shout in their sulphurous canopy.

The combat deepens. On, ye Brave,
Who rush to glory, or the grave!
Wave, Munich, all thy banners wave!
　　And charge with all thy chivalry!

Few, few shall part, where many meet!
The snow shall be their winding-sheet,
And every turf beneath their feet
    Shall be a soldier's sepulcher.

Thomas Campbell

* * *

THE DEFENCE OF FORT MCHENRY

O! say can you see, by the dawn's early light,
    What so proudly we hail'd at the twilight's last gleaming?
Whose broad stripes and bright stars through the perilous fight,
    O'er the ramparts we watch'd, were so gallantly streaming?
        And the rocket's red glare, the bombs bursting in air,
        Gave proof through the night that our flag was still
        there –
            O! say does that star-spangled banner yet wave
            O'er the land of the free and the home of the
            brave?

On the shore, dimly seen through the mists of the deep,
    Where the foe's haughty host in dread silence reposes,
What is that which the breeze o'er the towering steep,

As it fitfully blows, half conceals, half discloses?
    Now it catches the gleam of the morning's first
        doth wave
    In full glory reflected now shines on the stream –
    'Tis the star-spangled banner, O! long may it wave
    O'er the land of the free, and the home of the brave.

And where is that band who so vauntingly swore
    That the havoc of war and the battle's confusion,
A home and a country should leave us no more?
    Their blood has wash'd out their foul footsteps' pollution.
    No refuge could save the hireling and slave,
    From the terror of flight or the gloom of the grave;
      And the star-spangled banner in triumph
        doth wave
      O'er the land of the free, and the home of the
        brave.

O! thus be it ever, when freemen shall stand
    Between their lov'd home and the war's desolation,
Blest with vict'ry and peace, may the heav'n-rescued land
    Praise the power that hath made and preserv'd us a
      nation.

Then conquer we must, when our cause it is just,
And this be our motto – 'In God is our trust.'
  And the star-spangled banner in triumph
   shall wave
  O'er the land of the free and the home of the
   brave.

Francis Scott Key

* * *

THE CHARGE OF THE LIGHT BRIGADE

I

Half a league, half a league,
  Half a league onward,
All in the valley of Death
  Rode the six hundred.
'Forward the Light Brigade!
Charge for the guns!' he said.
Into the valley of Death
  Rode the six hundred.

II

'Forward, the Light Brigade!'
Was there a man dismay'd?
Not tho' the soldier knew
      Someone had blunder'd.
Theirs not to make reply,
Theirs not to reason why,
Theirs but to do and die.
Into the valley of Death
      Rode the six hundred.

III

Cannon to right of them,
Cannon to left of them,
Cannon in front of them
      Volley'd and thunder'd;
Storm'd at with shot and shell,
Boldly they rode and well,
Into the jaws of Death,
Into the mouth of hell
      Rode the six hundred.

IV

Flash'd all their sabres bare,
Flash'd as they turn'd in air
Sabring the gunners there,
Charging an army, while
    All the world wonder'd.
Plunged in the battery-smoke
Right thro' the line they broke;
Cossack and Russian
Reel'd from the sabre-stroke
    Shatter'd and sunder'd.
Then they rode back, but not,
    Not the six hundred.

V

Cannon to right of them,
Cannon to left of them,
Cannon behind them
    Volley'd and thunder'd;
Storm'd at with shot and shell,
While horse and hero fell,
They that had fought so well
Came thro' the jaws of Death,

Back from the mouth of hell,
All that was left of them,
    Left of six hundred.

VI

When can their glory fade?
O the wild charge they made!
    All the world wondered.
Honour the charge they made,
Honour the Light Brigade,
Noble six hundred!

Alfred, Lord Tennyson

* * *

THE ARTILLERYMAN'S VISION

While my wife at my side lies slumbering, and the wars are over
    long,
And my head on the pillow rests at home, and the vacant
    midnight passes,
And through the stillness, through the dark, I hear, just hear, the
    breath of my infant,

There in the room, as I wake from sleep, this vision presses upon
    me:

The engagement opens there and then, in fantasy unreal;

The skirmishers begin – they crawl cautiously ahead – I hear the
    irregular snap! snap!

I hear the sounds of the different missiles – the short *t-h-t! t-h-t!*
    of the rifle balls;

I see the shells exploding, leaving small white clouds – I hear the
    great shells shrieking as they pass;

The grape, like the hum and whirr of wind through the trees,
    (quick, tumultuous, now the contest rages!)

All the scenes at the batteries themselves rise in detail before me
    again;

The crashing and smoking – the pride of the men in their pieces;

The chief gunner ranges and sights his piece, and selects a fuse
    of the right time;

After firing, I see him lean aside, and look eagerly off to note the
    effect;

 – Elsewhere I hear the cry of a regiment charging – (the young
    colonel leads himself this time, with brandish'd sword);

I see the gaps cut by the enemy's volleys, (quickly fill'd up, no
    delay);

I breathe the suffocating smoke – then the flat clouds hover low,
    concealing all;

Now a strange lull comes for a few seconds, not a shot fired on
   either side;
Then resumed, the chaos louder than ever, with eager calls, and
   orders of officers;
While from some distant part of the field the wind wafts to my
   ears a shout of applause, (some special success);
And ever the sound of the cannon, far or near, (rousing, even in
   dreams, a devilish exultation, and all the old mad joy, in the
   depths of my soul);
And ever the hastening of infantry shifting positions – batteries,
   cavalry, moving hither and thither;
(The falling, dying, I heed not – the wounded, dripping and red,
   I heed not – some to the rear are hobbling);
Grime, heat, rush – aid-de-camps galloping by, or on a full run;
With the patter of small arms, the warning s-s-t of the rifles,
   (these in my vision I hear or see),
And bombs bursting in air, and at night the vari-color'd rockets.

Walt Whitman

HE FOUGHT LIKE THOSE WHO'VE NOUGHT TO LOSE

He fought like those Who've nought to lose—
Bestowed Himself to Balls
As One who for a further Life
Had not a further Use—

Invited Death—with bold attempt —
But Death was Coy of Him
As Other Men, were Coy of Death—
To Him—to live—was Doom—

His Comrades, shifted like the Flakes
When Gusts reverse the Snow—
But He—was left alive Because
Of Greediness to die—

Emily Dickinson

Into Battle

The naked earth is warm with Spring,
    And with green grass and bursting trees
Leans to the sun's gaze glorying,
    And quivers in the sunny breeze;

And life is colour and warmth and light,
    And a striving evermore for these;
And he is dead who will not fight;
    And who dies fighting has increase.

The fighting man shall from the sun
    Take warmth, and life from the glowing earth;
Speed with the light-foot winds to run,
    And with the trees to newer birth;
And find, when fighting shall be done,
    Great rest, and fullness after dearth.

All the bright company of Heaven
    Hold him in their high comradeship,
The Dog-Star, and the Sisters Seven,
    Orion's Belt and sworded hip.

The woodland trees that stand together,
    They stand to him each one a friend;
They gently speak in the windy weather;
    They guide to valley and ridge's end.

The kestrel hovering by day,
    And the little owls that call by night,
Bid him be swift and keen as they,
    As keen of ear, as swift of sight.

The blackbird sings to him, 'Brother, brother,
    If this be the last song you shall sing,
Sing well, for you may not sing another;
    Brother, sing.'

In dreary, doubtful, waiting hours,
    Before the brazen frenzy starts,
The horses show him nobler powers;
    O patient eyes, courageous hearts!

And when the burning moment breaks,
    And all things else are out of mind,
And only joy of battle takes
    Him by the throat, and makes him blind,

Through joy and blindness he shall know,
    Not caring much to know, that still
Nor lead nor steel shall reach him, so
    That it be not the Destined Will.

The thundering line of battle stands,
    And in the air death moans and sings;
But Day shall clasp him with strong hands,
    And Night shall fold him in soft wings.

Julian Grenfell

* * *

EXPOSURE

Our brains ache, in the merciless iced east winds that knife
    us...
Wearied we keep awake because the night is silent...
Low drooping flares confuse our memory of the salient...
Worried by silence, sentries whisper, curious, nervous,
But nothing happens.

Watching, we hear the mad gusts tugging on the wire.
Like twitching agonies of men among its brambles.

Northward incessantly, the flickering gunnery rumbles,
Far off, like a dull rumour of some other war.
  What are we doing here?

The poignant misery of dawn begins to grow
We only know war lasts, rain soaks, and clouds sag stormy.
Dawn massing in the east her melancholy army
Attacks once more in ranks on shivering ranks of gray,
  But nothing happens.

Sudden successive flights of bullets streak the silence.
Less deadly than the air that shudders black with snow,
With sidelong flowing flakes that flock, pause and renew,
We watch them wandering up and down the wind's
  nonchalance,
  But nothing happens.

Pale flakes with lingering stealth come feeling for our faces
We cringe in holes, back on forgotten dreams, and stare, snow-
  dazed,
Deep into grassier ditches. So we drowse, sun-dozed,
Littered with blossoms trickling where the blackbird fusses.
  Is it that we are dying?

Slowly our ghosts drag home: glimpsing the sunk fires glozed
With crusted dark-red jewels; crickets jingle there;
For hours the innocent mice rejoice: the house is theirs;
Shutters and doors all closed: on us the doors are closed
        We turn back to our dying.

Since we believe not otherwise can kind fires burn;
Now ever suns smile true on child, or field, or fruit.
For God's invincible spring our love is made afraid;
Therefore, not loath, we lie out here; therefore were born,
        For love of God seems dying.

Tonight, His frost will fasten on this mud and us,
Shrivelling many hands and puckering foreheads crisp.
The burying-party, picks and shovels in their shaking grasp,
Pause over half-known faces. All their eyes are ice,
        But nothing happens.

Wilfred Owen

THE ARMED LINER

The dull gray paint of war
Covering the shining brass and gleaming decks
That once re-echoed to the steps of youth.
That was before
The storms of destiny made ghastly wrecks
Of peace, the Right of Truth.
Impromptu dances, colored lights and laughter,
Lovers watching the phosphorescent waves,
Now gaping guns, a whistling shell; and after
So mans wandering graves.

H. Smalley Sarson

* * *

SPRING OFFENSIVE

Halted against the shade of a last hill,
They fed, and lying easy, were at ease
And, finding comfortable chest and knees
Carelessly slept. But many there stood still
To face the stark, blank sky beyond the ridge,
Knowing their feet had come to the end of the world.

Marvelling they stood, and watched the long grass swirled
By the May breeze, murmurous with wasp and midge,
For though the summer oozed into their veins
Like the injected drug for their bones' pains,
Sharp on their souls hung the imminent line of grass,
Fearfully flashed the sky's mysterious glass.

Hour after hour they ponder in the warm field, –
And the far valley behind, where the buttercups
Had blessed with gold their slow boots coming up,
When even the little brambles would not yield
But clutched and clung to them like sorrowing hands.
They breathe like trees unstirred.

Till like a cold gust thrilled the little word
At which each body and its soul begird
And tighten them for battle. No alarms
Of bugles, no high flags, no clamorous haste, –
Only a lift and flare of eyes that faced
The sun, like a friend with whom their love is done.
O larger shone that smile against the sun, –
Mightier than his whose bounty these have spurned.

So, soon they topped the hill, and raced together
Over an open stretch of herb and heather
Exposed. And instantly the whole sky burned
With fury against them; earth set sudden cups
In thousands for their blood; and the green slope
Chasmed and steepened sheer to infinite space.

Of them who running on that last high place
Leapt to swift unseen bullets, or went up
On the hot blast and fury of hell's upsurge,
Or plunged and fell away past this world's verge,
Some say God caught them even before they fell.

But what say such as from existence' brink
Ventured but drave too swift to sink,
The few who rushed in the body to enter hell,
And there outfiending all its fiend and flames
With superhuman inhumanities,
Long-famous glories, immemorial shames –
And crawling slowly back, have by degrees
Regained cool peaceful air in wonder –
Why speak not they of comrades that went under?

Wilfred Owen

To Germany

You are blind like us. Your hurt no man designed,
And no man claimed the conquest of your land.
But gropers both through fields of thought confined,
We stumble and we do not understand.
You only saw your future bigly planned,
And we, the tapering paths of our own mind,
And in each other's dearest ways we stand,
And hiss and hate. And the blind fight the blind.

When it is peace, then we may view again
With new-won eyes each other's truer form
And wonder. Grown more loving-kind and warm
We'll grasp firm hands and laugh at the old pain,
When it is peace. But until peace, the storm,
The darkness and the thunder and the rain.

Charles Hamilton Sorley

BREAK OF DAY IN THE TRENCHES

The darkness crumbles away.
It is the same old druid Time as ever,
Only a live thing leaps my hand,
A queer sardonic rat,
As I pull the parapet's poppy
To stick behind my ear.
Droll rat, they would shoot you if they knew
Your cosmopolitan sympathies.
Now you have touched this English hand
You will do the same to a German
Soon, no doubt, if it be your pleasure
To cross the sleeping green between.
It seems you inwardly grin as you pass
Strong eyes, fine limbs, haughty athletes,
Less chanced than you for life,
Bonds to the whims of murder,
Sprawled in the bowels of the earth,
The torn fields of France.
What do you see in our eyes
At the shrieking iron and flame
Hurled through still heavens?
What quaver – what heart aghast?
Poppies whose roots are in man's veins

Drop, and are ever dropping;
But mine in my ear is safe –
Just a little white with the dust.

Isaac Rosenberg

* * *

PAIN

Pain, pain continual; pain unending;
Hard even to the roughest, but to those
Hungry for beauty… Not the wisest knows,
Nor most pitiful-hearted, what the wending
Of one hour's way meant. Grey monotony lending
Weight to the grey skies, grey mud where goes
An army of grey bedrenched scarecrows in rows
Careless at last of cruellest Fate-sending.
Seeing the pitiful eyes of men foredone,
Or horses shot, too tired merely to stir,
Dying in shell-holes both, slain by the mud.
Men broken, shrieking even to hear a gun. –
Till pain grinds down, or lethargy numbs her,
The amazed heart cries angrily out on God.

Ivor Gurney

The Shell

Shrieking its message the flying death
Cursed the resisting air,
Then buried its nose by a battered church,
A skeleton gaunt and bare.

The brains of science, the money of fools
Had fashioned an iron slave
Destined to kill, yet the futile end
Was a child's uprooted grave.

H. Smalley Sarson

* * *

Bombardment

The town has opened to the sun.
Like a flat red lily with a million petals
She unfolds, she comes undone.

A sharp sky brushes upon
The myriad glittering chimney-tips
As she gently exhales to the sun.

Hurrying creatures run
Down the labyrinth of the sinister flower.
What is it they shun?

A dark bird falls from the sun.
It curves in a rush to the heart of the vast
Flower: the day has begun.

D. H. Lawrence

* * *

FULL MOON AT TIERZ: BEFORE THE STORMING OF HUESCA

The past, a glacier, gripped the mountain wall,
And time was inches, dark was all.
But here it scales the end of the range,
The dialectic's point of change,
Crashes in light and minutes to its fall.

Time present is a cataract whose force
Breaks down the banks even at its source
And history forming in our hands
Not plasticine but roaring sands,
Yet we must swing it to its final course.

The intersecting lines that cross both ways,
Time future, has no image in space,
Crooked as the road that we must tread,
Straight as our bullets fly ahead.
We are the future. The last fight let us face.

John Cornford

THE HOME FRONT

One noonday, at my window in the town,
  I saw a sight – saddest that eyes can see –
  Young soldiers marching lustily
  Unto the wars,
With fifes, and flags in mottoed pageantry...

On Hearing the Drum

I hate that drum's discordant sound,
Parading round, and round, and round:
To thoughtless youth it pleasure yields,
And lures from cities and from fields,
To sell their liberty for charms
Of tawdry lace and glittering arms;
And when Ambition's voice commands,
To march, and fight, and fall in foreign lands.

I hate that drum's discordant sound,
Parading round, and round, and round:
To me it talks of ravaged plains,
And burning towns and ruin'd swains,
And mangled limbs, and dying groans,
And widows' tears, and orphans' moans,
And all that Misery's hand bestows,
To fill a catalogue of woes.

John Scott

MOTHER AND POET

I

Dead! One of them shot by the sea in the east,
    And one of them shot in the west by the sea.
Dead! both my boys! When you sit at the feast
    And are wanting a great song for Italy free,
        Let none look at *me*!

II

    Yet I was a poetess only last year,
    And good at my art, for a woman, men said;
But *this* woman, *this*, who is agonized here,
      – The east sea and west sea rhyme on in her head
        For ever instead.

III

What art can a woman be good at? Oh, vain!
    What art *is* she good at, but hurting her breast
With the milk-teeth of babes, and a smile at the pain?
Ah boys, how you hurt! you were strong as you pressed,
      And I proud, by that test.

IV

What art's for a woman? To hold on her knees
      Both darlings! to feel all their arms round her throat,
Cling, strangle a little! to sew by degrees
      And 'broider the long-clothes and neat little coat;
          To dream and to doat.

V

To teach them... It stings there! *I* made them indeed
      Speak plain the word *country*. *I* taught them, no doubt,
That a country's a thing men should die for at need.
      I prated of liberty, rights, and about
          The tyrant cast out.

VI

And when their eyes flashed... O my beautiful eyes!...
      I exulted; nay, let them go forth at the wheels
Of the guns, and denied not. But then the surprise
      When one sits quite alone! Then one weeps, then one
        kneels!
        God, how the house feels!

VII

At first, happy news came, in gay letters moiled
      With my kisses – of camp-life and glory, and how
They both loved me; and, soon coming home to be spoiled
      In return would fan off every fly from my brow
          With their green laurel-bough.

VIII

Then was triumph at Turin: 'Ancona was free!'
      And someone came out of the cheers in the street,
With a face pale as stone, to say something to me.
      My Guido was dead! I fell down at his feet,
          While they cheered in the street.

IX

I bore it; friends soothed me; my grief looked sublime
      As the ransom of Italy. One boy remained
To be leant on and walked with, recalling the time
      When the first grew immortal, while both of us
        strained
          To the height he had gained.

X

And letters still came, shorter, sadder, more strong,
      Writ now but in one hand, 'I was not to faint –
One loved me for two – would be with me ere long :
      And *Viva l'Italia!* – he died for, our saint,
        Who forbids our complaint.'

XI

My Nanni would add, 'he was safe, and aware
      Of a presence that turned off the balls, – was imprest
It was Guido himself, who knew what I could bear,
      And how 'twas impossible, quite dispossessed,
        To live on for the rest.'

XII

On which, without pause, up the telegraph line
      Swept smoothly the next news from Gaeta: Shot.
Tell his mother. Ah, ah, 'his', 'their' mother – not 'mine',
      No voice says 'My mother' again to me. What!
        You think Guido forgot?

XIII

Are souls straight so happy that, dizzy with Heaven,
      They drop earth's affections, conceive not of woe?

I think not. Themselves were too lately forgiven
      Through *that* Love and Sorrow which reconciled so
        The Above and Below.

XIV

O Christ of the five wounds, who look'dst through the dark
      To the face of Thy mother! consider, I pray,
How we common mothers stand desolate, mark,
      Whose sons, not being Christs, die with eyes turned
      away,
        And no last word to say!

XV

Both boys dead? but that's out of nature. We all
      Have been patriots, yet each house must always keep
      one.
'Twere imbecile, hewing out roads to a wall;
      And, when Italy's made, for what end is it done
        If we have not a son?

XVI

Ah, ah, ah! when Gaeta's taken, what then?
      When the fair wicked queen sits no more at her sport

Of the fire-balls of death crashing souls out of men?
    When the guns of Cavalli with final retort
        Have cut the game short?

XVII

When Venice and Rome keep their new jubilee,
    When your flag takes all heaven for its white, green,
        and red,
When *you* have your country from mountain to sea,
    When King Victor has Italy's crown on his head,
        (And *I* have my Dead) –

XVIII

What then? Do not mock me. Ah, ring your bells low,
    And burn your lights faintly! *My* country is *there*,
Above the star pricked by the last peak of snow:
    My Italy's *there*, with my brave civic Pair,
        To disfranchise despair!

XIX

Forgive me. Some women bear children in strength,
    And bite back the cry of their pain in self-scorn;
But the birth-pangs of nations will wring us at length

Into wail such as this – and we sit on forlorn
When the man-child is born.

XX

Dead! One of them shot by the sea in the east,
    And one of them shot in the west by the sea.
Both! both my boys! If in keeping the feast
    You want a great song for your Italy free,
        Let none look at *me*!

Elizabeth Barrett Browning

* * *

When I was Small, a Woman Died

When I was small, a woman died.
Today her only boy
Went up from the Potomac,
His face all victory,

To look at her; how slowly
The seasons must have turned
Till bullets clipt an angle,
And he passed quickly round!

If pride shall be in Paradise
I never can decide;
Of their imperial conduct,
No person testified.

But proud in apparition,
That woman and her boy
Pass back and forth before my brain,
As ever in the sky.

Emily Dickinson

* * *

COME UP FROM THE FIELDS, FATHER

I

Come up from the fields, father, here's a letter from our Pete;
And come to the front door, mother – here's a letter from thy
dear son.

II

Lo, 'tis autumn;
Lo, where the trees, deeper green, yellower and redder,
Cool and sweeten Ohio's villages, with leaves fluttering in the
moderate wind;

Where apples ripe in the orchards hang, and grapes on the
    trellis'd vines;
(Smell you the smell of the grapes on the vines?
Smell you the buckwheat, where the bees were lately buzzing?)

Above all, lo, the sky, so calm, so transparent after the rain, and
    with wondrous clouds;
Below, too, all calm, all vital and beautiful – and the farm
    prospers well.

III

Down in the fields all prospers well;
But now from the fields come, father – come at the daughter's
    call;
And come to the entry, mother – to the front door come, right
    away.

Fast as she can she hurries – something ominous – her steps
    trembling;
She does not tarry to smoothe her hair, nor adjust her cap.

Open the envelope quickly;
O this is not our son's writing, yet his name is sign'd;

O a strange hand writes for our dear son – O stricken mother's
soul!

All swims before her eyes – flashes with black – she catches the
main words only;

Sentences broken – *gun-shot wound in the breast, cavalry skirmish,
taken to hospital,*

At present low, but will soon be better.

IV

Ah, now, the single figure to me,

Amid all teeming and wealthy Ohio, with all its cities and
farms,

Sickly white in the face, and dull in the head, very faint,

By the jamb of a door leans.

Grieve not so, dear mother, (the just-grown daughter speaks
through her sobs;

The little sisters huddle around, speechless and dismay'd);

See, dearest mother, the letter says Pete will soon be better.

V

Alas, poor boy, he will never be better, (nor maybe needs to be
better, that brave and simple soul);

While they stand at home at the door, he is dead already;
The only son is dead.

But the mother needs to be better;
She, with thin form, presently drest in black;
By day her meals untouch'd – then at night fitfully sleeping,
  often waking,
In the midnight waking, weeping, longing with one deep
  longing,
O that she might withdraw unnoticed – silent from life, escape
  and withdraw,
To follow, to seek, to be with her dear dead son.

Walt Whitman

* * *

BALL'S BLUFF: A REVERIE

One noonday, at my window in the town,
  I saw a sight – saddest that eyes can see –
  Young soldiers marching lustily
    Unto the wars,
With fifes, and flags in mottoed pageantry;

While all the porches, walks, and doors
Were rich with ladies cheering royally.

They moved like Juny morning on the wave,
      Their hearts were fresh as clover in its prime
      (It was the breezy summer time),
          Life throbbed so strong,
How should they dream that Death in rosy clime
      Would come to thin their shining throng?
Youth feels immortal, like the gods sublime.

Weeks passed; and at my window, leaving bed,
      By nights I mused, of easeful sleep bereft,
      On those brave boys (Ah War! thy theft);
          Some marching feet
Found pause at last by cliffs Potomac cleft;
      Wakeful I mused, while in the street
Far footfalls died away till none were left.

Herman Melville

Your Letter, Lady, Came Too Late

Your letter, lady, came too late,
　　　For Heaven had claimed its own.
Ah, sudden change! From prison bars
　　　Unto the Great White Throne!
And yet, I think he would have stayed
　　　To live for his disdain,
Could he have read the careless words
　　　Which you have sent in vain.

So full of patience did he wait
　　　Through many a weary hour,
That o'er his simple soldier faith
　　　Not even death had power.
And you – did others whisper low
　　　Their homage in your ear,
As though among their shadowy throng
　　　His spirit had a peer.

I would that you were by me now,
　　　To draw the sheet aside,
And see how pure the look he wore
　　　The moment when he died.

The sorrow that you gave him
    Had left its weary trace,
As 'twere the shadow of the cross
    Upon his pallid face.

'Her love,' he said, 'could change for me
    The winter's cold to spring.'
Ah, trust of fickle maiden's love,
    Thou art a bitter thing!
For when these valleys bright in May
    Once more with blossoms wave,
The northern violets shall blow
    Above his humble grave.

Your dole of scanty words had been
    But one more pang to bear,
For him who kissed unto the last
    Your tress of golden hair.
I did not put it where he said,
    For when the angels come
I would not have them find the sign
    Of falsehood in the tomb.

I've seen your letter and I know
       The wiles that you have wrought
To win that noble heart of his,
       And gained it – cruel thought!
What lavish wealth men sometimes give
       For what is worthless all:
What manly bosoms beat for them
       In folly's falsest thrall.

You shall not pity him, for now
       His sorrow has an end,
Yet would that you could stand with me
       Beside my fallen friend.
And I forgive you for his sake
       As he – if it be given –
May even be pleading grace for you
       Before the court of heaven.

Tonight the cold wind whistles by
       As I my vigil keep
Within the prison dead house, where
       Few mourners come to weep.
A rude plank coffin holds his form,

Yet death exalts his face
And I would rather see him thus
    Than clasped in your embrace.

Tonight your home may shine with lights
    And ring with merry song,
And you be smiling as if your soul
    Had done no deadly wrong.
Your hand so fair that none would think
    It penned these words of pain;
Your skin so white – would God your heart
    Were half as free from stain.

I'd rather be my comrade dead,
    Than you in life supreme:
For yours the sinner's waking dread,
    And his the martyr's dream.
Whom serve we in this life, we serve
    In that which is to come:
He chose his way, you yours; let God
    Pronounce the fitting doom.

W. S. Hawkins

Do Not Weep, Maiden, For War is Kind

Do not weep, maiden, for war is kind.
Because your lover threw wild hands toward the sky
And the affrighted steed ran on alone,
Do not weep.
War is kind.

Hoarse, booming drums of the regiment,
Little souls who thirst for fight,
These men were born to drill and die.
The unexplained glory flies above them,
Great is the battle-god, great, and his kingdom –
A field where a thousand corpses lie.

Do not weep, babe, for war is kind.
Because your father tumbled in the yellow trenches,
Raged at his breast, gulped and died,
Do not weep.
War is kind.

Swift blazing flag of the regiment,
Eagle with crest of red and gold,
These men were born to drill and die.

Point for them the virtue of slaughter,
Make plain to them the excellence of killing
And a field where a thousand corpses lie.

Mother whose heart hung humble as a button
On the bright splendid shroud of your son,
Do not weep.
War is kind.

Stephen Crane

* * *

CHRISTMAS BELLS

I heard the bells on Christmas Day
Their old familiar carols play,
And wild and sweet
The words repeat
Of peace on earth, goodwill to men!

And thought how, as the day had come,
The belfries of all Christendom
Had rolled along

The unbroken song
Of peace on earth, goodwill to men!

Till, ringing, singing on its way,
The world revolved from night to day,
A voice, a chime
A chant sublime
Of peace on earth, goodwill to men!

Then from each black accursed mouth
The cannon thundered in the South,
And with the sound
The carols drowned
Of peace on earth, goodwill to men!

It was as if an earthquake rent
The hearth-stones of a continent,
And made forlorn
The households born
Of peace on earth, goodwill to men!

And in despair I bowed my head;
'There is no peace on earth,' I said;
'For hate is strong,

And mocks the song
Of peace on earth, goodwill to men!'

Then pealed the bells more loud and deep:
'God is not dead; nor doth he sleep!
    The Wrong shall fail,
    The Right prevail,
With peace on earth, goodwill to men!'

Henry Wadsworth Longfellow

* * *

IT FEELS A SHAME TO BE ALIVE

It feels a shame to be Alive—
When Men so brave—are dead—
One envies the Distinguished Dust—
Permitted—such a Head—

The Stone—that tells defending Whom
This Spartan put away
What little of Him we—possessed
In Pawn for Liberty—

The price is great—Sublimely paid—
Do we deserve—a Thing—
That lives—like Dollars—must be piled
Before we may obtain?

Are we that wait —sufficient worth—
That such Enormous Pearl
As life—dissolved be—for Us—
In Battle's—horrid Bowl?

It may be—a Renown to live—
I think the Man who die—
Those unsustained—Saviors—
Present Divinity—

Emily Dickinson

* * *

TOMMY

I went into a public-'ouse to get a pint o' beer,
The publican 'e up an' sez, 'We serve no red-coats here.'
The girls be'ind the bar they laughed an' giggled fit to die,

I outs into the street again an' to myself sez I:

> O it's Tommy this, an' Tommy that, an' 'Tommy, go away';
> But it's 'Thank you, Mister Atkins', when the band
> begins to play,
> The band begins to play, my boys, the band begins to
> play,
> O it's 'Thank you, Mister Atkins', when the band begins
> to play.

I went into a theatre as sober as could be,
They gave a drunk civilian room, but 'adn't none for me;
They sent me to the gallery or round the music-'alls,
But when it comes to fightin', Lord! They'll shove me in the
stalls!

> For it's Tommy this, an' Tommy that, an' 'Tommy, wait
> outside';
> But it's 'Special train for Atkins' when the trooper's on
> the tide,
> The troopship's on the tide, my boys, the troopship's on
> the tide,
> O it's 'Special train for Atkins' when the trooper's on
> the tide.

Yes, makin' mock o' uniforms that guard you while you
    sleep
Is cheaper than them uniforms, an' they're starvation cheap;
An' hustlin' drunken soldiers when they're goin' large a bit
Is five times better business than paradin' in full kit.
        Then it's Tommy this, an' Tommy that, an' 'Tommy,
           'ow's yer soul?'
        But it's 'Thin red line of 'eroes' when the drums begin
           to roll,
        The drums begin to roll, my boys, the drums begin
           to roll,
        O it's 'Thin red line of 'eroes' when the drums begin
           to roll.
We aren't no thin red 'eroes, nor we aren't no blackguards
    too,
But single men in barricks, most remarkable like you;
An' if sometimes our conduck isn't all your fancy paints,
Why, single men in barricks don't grow into plaster saints;
        While it's Tommy this, an' Tommy that, an' 'Tommy,
           fall be'ind',
        But it's 'Please to walk in front, sir', when there's
           trouble in the wind,

There's trouble in the wind, my boys, there's trouble
in the wind,
O it's 'Please to walk in front, sir', when there's
trouble in the wind.

You talk o' better food for us, an' schools, an' fires, an' all:
We'll wait for extry rations if you treat us rational.
Don't mess about the cook-room slops, but prove it to our
face
The Widow's Uniform is not the soldier-man's disgrace.
For it's Tommy this, an' Tommy that, an' 'Chuck him
out, the brute!'
But it's 'Saviour of 'is country' when the guns begin to
shoot;
An' it's Tommy this, an' Tommy that, an' anything
you please;
An' Tommy ain't a bloomin' fool – you bet that
Tommy sees.

Rudyard Kipling

A Wife in London

(December, 1899)

I

She sits in the tawny vapour
  That the Thames-side lanes have uprolled,
  Behind whose webby fold on fold
Like a waning taper
  The street-lamp glimmers cold.

A messenger's knock cracks smartly,
  Flashed news is in her hand
  Of meaning it dazes to understand
Though shaped so shortly:
  He – has fallen – in the far South Land…

II

'Tis the morrow; the fog hangs thicker,
  The postman nears and goes:
  A letter is brought whose lines disclose
By the firelight flicker
  His hand, whom the worm now knows:

Fresh – firm – penned in highest feather –
    Page-full of his hoped return,
    And of home-planned jaunts by brake and burn
In the summer weather,
    And of new love that they would learn.

Thomas Hardy

* * *

THE ISLANDERS

No doubt but ye are the People – your throne is above the King's.
Whoso speaks in your presence must say acceptable things:
Bowing the head in worship, bending the knee in fear –
Bringing the word well smoothen – such as a King should hear.

Fenced by your careful fathers, ringed by your leaden seas,
Long did ye wake in quiet and long lie down at ease;
Till ye said of Strife, 'What is it?' of the Sword, 'It is far from
    our ken':
Till ye made a sport of your shrunken hosts and a toy of your
    armed men.
Ye stopped your ears to the warning – ye would neither look
    nor heed –

Ye set your leisure before their toil and your lusts above their
   need.

Because of your witless learning and your beasts of warren and
   chase,

Ye grudged your sons to their service and your fields for their
   camping-place.

Ye forced them to glean in the highways the straw for the
   bricks they brought;

Ye forced them follow in byways the craft that ye never taught.

Ye hindered and hampered and crippled; ye thrust out of sight
   and away

Those that would serve you for honour and those that served
   you for pay.

Then were the judgments loosened; then was your shame
   revealed,

At the hands of a little people, few but apt in the field.

Yet ye were saved by a remnant (and your land's long-
   suffering star),

When your strong men cheered in their millions while your
   striplings went to the war.

Sons of the sheltered city – unmade, unhandled, unmeet –

Ye pushed them raw to the battle as ye picked them raw from
   the street.

And what did ye look they should compass? Warcraft learned
    in a breath,
Knowledge unto occasion at the first far view of Death?
So? And ye train your horses and the dogs ye feed and prize?
How are the beasts more worthy than the souls, your sacrifice?
But ye said, 'Their valour shall show them'; but ye said, 'The
    end is close.'
And ye sent them comfits and pictures to help them harry your
    foes:
And ye vaunted your fathomless power, and ye flaunted your
    iron pride,
Ere – ye fawned on the Younger Nations for the men who
    could shoot and ride!
Then ye returned to your trinkets; then ye contented your souls
With the flannelled fools at the wicket or the muddied oafs at
    the goals.
Given to strong delusion, wholly believing a lie,
Ye saw that the land lay fenceless, and ye let the months go by
Waiting some easy wonder, hoping some saving sign
Idle – openly idle – in the lee of the forespent Line.
Idle – except for your boasting – and what is your boasting
    worth
If ye grudge a year of service to the lordliest life on earth?

Ancient, effortless, ordered, cycle on cycle set,

Life so long untroubled, that ye who inherit forget

It was not made with the mountains, it is not one with the
deep.

Men, not gods, devised it. Men, not gods, must keep.

Men, not children, servants, or kinsfolk called from afar,

But each man born in the Island broke to the matter of war.

Soberly and by custom taken and trained for the same,

Each man born in the Island entered at youth to the game –

As it were almost cricket, not to be mastered in haste,

But after trial and labour, by temperance, living chaste.

As it were almost cricket – as it were even your play,

Weighed and pondered and worshipped, and practised day
and day.

So ye shall bide sure-guarded when the restless lightnings
wake

In the womb of the blotting war-cloud, and the pallid nations
quake.

So, at the haggard trumpets, instant your soul shall leap

Forthright, accoutred, accepting – alert from the wells of sleep.

So at the threat ye shall summon – so at the need ye shall send

Men, not children or servants, tempered and taught to the end;

Cleansed of servile panic, slow to dread or despise,

Humble because of knowledge, mighty by sacrifice.

But ye say, 'It will mar our comfort.' Ye say, 'It will minish our
  trade.'

Do ye wait for the spattered shrapnel ere ye learn how a gun is
  laid?

For the low, red glare to southward when the raided coast-
  towns burn?

(Light ye shall have on that lesson, but little time to learn.)

Will ye pitch some white pavilion, and lustily even the odds,

With nets and hoops and mallets, with rackets and bats and
  rods?

Will the rabbit war with your foemen – the red deer horn them
  for hire?

Your kept cock – pheasant keep you? – he is master of many a
  shire.

Arid, aloof, incurious, unthinking, unthanking, gelt,

Will ye loose your schools to flout them till their brow-beat
  columns melt?

Will ye pray them or preach them, or print them, or ballot them
  back from your shore?

Will your workmen issue a mandate to bid them strike no more?

Will ye rise and dethrone your rulers? (Because ye were idle
  both?

Pride by Insolence chastened? Indolence purged by Sloth?)
No doubt but ye are the People; who shall make you afraid?
Also your gods are many; no doubt but your gods shall aid.
Idols of greasy altars built for the body's ease;
Proud little brazen Baals and talking fetishes;
Teraphs of sept and party and wise wood-pavement gods –
These shall come down to the battle and snatch you from
    under the rods?
From the gusty, flickering gun-roll with viewless salvoes rent,
And the pitted hail of the bullets that tell not whence they were
    sent.
When ye are ringed as with iron, when ye are scourged as with
    whips,
When the meat is yet in your belly, and the boast is yet on your
    lips;
When ye go forth at morning and the noon beholds you broke,
Ere ye lie down at even, your remnant, under the yoke?

No doubt but ye are the People – absolute, strong, and wise;
Whatever your heart has desired ye have not withheld from your eyes.
On your own heads, in your own hands, the sin and the saving lies!

Rudyard Kipling

In Time of 'The Breaking of the Nations'

Only a man harrowing clods
    In a slow silent walk,
With an old horse that stumbles and nods
    Half asleep as they stalk.

Only thin smoke without flame
    From the heaps of couch grass:
Yet this will go onward the same
    Though Dynasties pass.

Yonder a maid and her wight
    Come whispering by;
War's annals will fade into night
    Ere their story die.

Thomas Hardy

On Being Asked for a War Poem

I think it better that in times like these
A poet keep his mouth shut, for in truth
We have no gift to set a statesman right;
He has had enough of meddling who can please
A young girl in the indolence of her youth,
Or an old man upon a winter's night.

W. B. Yeats

* * *

Glory of Women

You love us when we're heroes, home on leave,
Or wounded in a mentionable place.
You worship decorations; you believe
That chivalry redeems the war's disgrace.
You make us shells. You listen with delight,
By tales of dirt and danger fondly thrilled.
You crown our distant ardours while we fight,
And mourn our laurelled memories when we're killed.
You can't believe that British troops 'retire'
When hell's last horror breaks them, and they run,

Trampling the terrible corpses – blind with blood.
O German mother dreaming by the fire,
While you are knitting socks to send your son
His face is trodden deeper in the mud.

Siegfried Sassoon

* * *

CHANNEL FIRING

That night your great guns, unawares,
Shook all our coffins as we lay,
And broke the chancel window-squares,
We thought it was the Judgment-day

And sat upright. While drearisome
Arose the howl of wakened hounds:
The mouse let fall the altar-crumb,
The worms drew back into the mounds,

The glebe cow drooled. Till God called, 'No;
It's gunnery practice out at sea
Just as before you went below;
The world is as it used to be:

'All nations striving strong to make
Red war yet redder. Mad as hatters
They do no more for Christés sake
Than you who are helpless in such matters.

'That this is not the judgment-hour
For some of them's a blessed thing,
For if it were they'd have to scour
Hell's floor for so much threatening…

'Ha, ha. It will be warmer when
I blow the trumpet (if indeed
I ever do; for you are men,
And rest eternal sorely need).'

So down we lay again. 'I wonder,
Will the world ever saner be,'
Said one, 'than when He sent us under
In our indifferent century!'

And many a skeleton shook his head.
'Instead of preaching forty year,'
My neighbour Parson Thirdly said,
'I wish I had stuck to pipes and beer.'

Again the guns disturbed the hour,
Roaring their readiness to avenge,
As far inland as Stourton Tower,
And Camelot, and starlit Stonehenge.

Thomas Hardy

* * *

THE SONG OF SHEFFIELD

Shells, shells, shells!
The song of the city of steel;
Hammer and turn, and file,
Furnace, and lathe, and wheel.
Tireless machinery,
Man's ingenuity,
Making a way for the martial devil's meal.

Shells, shells, shells!
Out of the furnace blaze;
Roll, roll, roll,
Into the workshop's maze.
Ruthless machinery
Boring eternally,
Boring a hole for the shattering charge that stays.

Shells, shells, shells!
The song of the city of steel;
List to the devil's mirth,
Hark to their laughter's peal:
Sheffield's machinery
Crushing humanity
Neath devil-ridden death's impassive heel.

Harold Beckh

* * *

TWO FINE LADIES

I saw two ladies in their car
  With seven Pekingese.
I know where your sisters sob
  The dragging hours away,
Where ever-toiling factories rob
  Children of their play.
Where squalid hovels like a scar
Hide Christ's humanities.
Two fine ladies in their car
  With seven Pekingese.

I have heard a mother cry
     Her anguishing distress
That her first-born had to die
     To please the passionless.
And I have watched your children mar
     Their beauty by disease
Two fine ladies in their car
     With seven Pekingese.

I know where your youth has died
In suffering and pain,
     That you might keep your honoured pride
To glory in your gain;
And I have watched an evening star
     Weep for your agonies.
Two fine ladies in their car
     With seven Pekingese.

I have smiled to hear you talk
     Of statesmanship and art,
I've watched your self-important walk
     And analysed your heart.

I know you for the fools you are
You puny vanities.
Two fine ladies in their car
With seven Pekingese.

H. Smalley Sarson

* * *

SMILE, SMILE, SMILE

Head to limp head, the sunk-eyed wounded scanned
Yesterday's *Mail*; the casualties (typed small)
And (large) Vast Booty from our Latest Haul.
Also, they read of Cheap Homes, not yet planned;
For, said the paper, 'When this war is done
The men's first instinct will be making homes.
Meanwhile their foremost need is aerodromes,
It being certain war has just begun.
Peace would do wrong to our undying dead, –
The sons we offered might regret they died
If we got nothing lasting in their stead.
We must be solidly indemnified.
Though all be worthy Victory which all bought,
We rulers sitting in this ancient spot

Would wrong our very selves if we forgot
The greatest glory will be theirs who fought,
Who kept this nation in integrity.'
Nation? – The half-limbed readers did not chafe
But smiled at one another curiously
Like secret men who know their secret safe.
(This is the thing they know and never speak,
That England one by one had fled to France,
Not many elsewhere now, save under France.)
Pictures of these broad smiles appear each week,
And people in whose voice real feeling rings
Say: How they smile! They're happy now, poor things.

Wilfred Owen

FIELDS OF DEATH

Who died on the wires, and hung there, one of two –
Who for his hours of life had chattered through
Infinite lovely chatter of Bucks accent:
Yet faced unbroken wires; stepped over, and went
A noble fool, faithful to his stripes – and ended.

THE WAR SONG OF DINAS VAWR

The mountain sheep are sweeter,
But the valley sheep are fatter;
We therefore deem'd it meeter
To carry off the latter.
We made an expedition;
We met an host and quell'd it;
We forced a strong position
And kill'd the men who held it.

On Dyfed's richest valley,
Where herds of kine were browsing,
We made a mighty sally,
To furnish our carousing.
Fierce warriors rush'd to meet us;
We met them, and o'erthrew them:
They struggled hard to beat us,
But we conquer'd them, and slew them.

As we drove our prize at leisure,
The king march'd forth to catch us:
His rage surpass'd all measure,
But his people could not match us.

He fled to his hall-pillars;
And, ere our force we led off,
Some sack'd his house and cellars,
While others cut his head off.

We there, in strife bewildering,
Spilt blood enough to swim in:
We orphan'd many children
And widow'd many women.
The eagles and the ravens
We glutted with our foemen:
The heroes and the cravens,
The spearmen and the bowmen.

We brought away from battle,
And much their land bemoan'd them,
Two thousand head of cattle
And the head of him who own'd them:
Ednyfed, King of Dyfed,
His head was borne before us;
His wine and beasts supplied our feasts,
And his overthrow, our chorus.

Thomas Love Peacock

ODE TO THE CAMBRO-BRITONS AND THEIR HARP, HIS BALLAD OF AGINCOURT

Fair stood the wind for France,
When we our sails advance;
Nor now to prove our chance
    Longer will tarry;
But putting to the main,
At Caux, the mouth of Seine,
With all his martial train
    Landed King Harry.

And taking many a fort,
Furnish'd in warlike sort,
Marcheth towards Agincourt
    In happy hour;
Skirmishing day by day
With those that stopp'd his way,
Where the French gen'ral lay
    With all his power.

Which, in his height of pride,
King Henry to deride,
His ransom to provide

To the King sending;
Which he neglects the while,
As from a nation vile
Yet with an angry smile
　　　Their fall portending.

And turning to his men
Quoth our brave Henry then:
'Though they to one be ten
　　　Be not amazed.
Yet have we well begun:
Battles so bravely won
Have ever to the sun
　　　By Fame been raised!

'And for myself,' quoth he,
'This my full rest shall be:
England ne'er mourn for me,
　　　Nor more esteem me;
Victor I will remain,
Or on this earth lie slain;
Never shall she sustain
　　　Loss to redeem me!

'Poitiers and Cressy tell
When most their pride did swell
Under our swords they fell;
    No less our skill is
Than when our grandsire great,
Claiming the regal seat,
By many a warlike feat
    Lopp'd the French lilies.'

The Duke of York so dread
The eager vaward led;
With the main Henry sped
    Amongst his henchmen:
Excester had the rear,
A braver man not there
O Lord, how hot they were
    On the false Frenchmen!

They now to fight are gone;
Armour on armour shone;
Drum now to drum did groan:
    To hear, was wonder;
That, with cries they make,

The very earth did shake;
Trumpet to trumpet spake,
  Thunder to thunder.

Well it thine age became,
O noble Erpingham,
Which didst the signal aim
  To our hid forces;
When, from a meadow by,
Like a storm suddenly,
The English archery
  Stuck the French horses

With Spanish yew so strong,
Arrows a cloth-yard long,
That like to serpents stung,
  Piercing the weather.
None from his fellow starts,
But playing manly parts,
And like true English hearts
  Stuck close together.

When down their bows they threw,
And forth their bilboes drew,

And on the French they flew,
    Not one was tardy;
Arms were from shoulders sent,
Scalps to the teeth were rent,
Down the French peasants went:
    Our men were hardy.

This while our noble King,
His broad sword brandishing,
Down the French host did ding,
    As to o'erwhelm it.
And many a deep wound lent,
His arms with blood besprent,
And many a cruel dent
    Bruised his helmet.

Gloster, that duke so good,
Next of the royal blood,
For famous England stood
    With his brave brother.
Clarence, in steel so bright,
Though but a maiden knight,

Yet in that furious fight
       Scarce such another!

Warwick in blood did wade,
Oxford the foe invade,
And cruel slaughter made,
       Still as they ran up.
Suffolk his axe did ply;
Beaumont and Willoughby
Bare them right doughtily;
       Ferrers and Fanhope.

Upon Saint Crispin's Day
Fought was this noble fray,
Which fame did not delay
       To England to carry.
O when shall English men
With such acts fill a pen,
Or England breed again
       Such a King Harry?

Michael Drayton

THE COLLEGE COLONEL

He rides at their head;
    A crutch by his saddle just slants in view,
One slung arm is in splints you see,
    Yet he guides his strong steed – how coldly too.

He brings his regiment home,
    Not as they filed two years before;
But a remnant half-tattered, and battered, and worn,
Like castaway sailors, who, stunned
    By the surf's loud roar,
    Their mates dragged back and seen no more, –
Again and again breast the surge,
    And at last crawl, spent, to shore.

A still rigidity and pale,
    An Indian aloofness, lones his brow;
He has lived a thousand years
Compressed in battle's pains and prayers,
    Marches and watches slow.

There are welcoming shouts and flags;
    Old men off hat to the Boy,
Wreaths from gay balconies fall at his feet,
    But to him – there comes alloy.

It is not that a leg is lost,
    It is not that an arm is maimed,
It is not that the fever has racked, –
    Self he has long disclaimed.

But all through the Seven Days' Fight,
    And deep in the Wilderness grim,
And in the field-hospital tent,
    And Petersburg crater, and dim
Lean brooding in Libby, there came –
    Ah heaven! – what *truth* to him!

Herman Melville

THE WOUND DRESSER

I

An old man bending I come among new faces,

Years looking backward resuming in answer to children,

Come tell us old man, as from young men and maidens that
love me,

(Arous'd and angry, I'd thought to beat the alarum, and urge
relentless war,

But soon my fingers fail'd me, my face droop'd and I resign'd
myself,

To sit by the wounded and soothe them, or silently watch the
dead;)

Years hence of these scenes, of these furious passions, these
chances,

Of unsurpass'd heroes (was one side so brave? the other was
equally brave;)

Now be witness again, paint the mightiest armies of earth,

Of those armies so rapid, so wondrous what saw you to tell us?

What stays with you latest and deepest? of curious panics,

Of hard-fought engagements or sieges tremendous what
deepest remains?

II

O maidens and young men I love and that love me,

What you ask of my days those the strangest and sudden your
talking recalls,

Soldier alert I arrive after a long march cover'd with sweat and
dust,

In the nick of time I come, plunge in the fight, loudly shout in
the rush of successful charge,

Enter the captur'd works – yet lo, like a swift-running river
they fade,

Pass and are gone they fade – I dwell not on soldiers' perils or
soldiers' joys

(Both I remember well – many the hardships, few the joys, yet I
was content).

But in silence, in dreams' projections,

While the world of gain and appearance and mirth goes on,

So soon what is over forgotten, and waves wash the imprints
off the sand,

With hinged knees returning I enter the doors (while for you
up there,

Whoever you are, follow without noise and be of strong heart).

Bearing the bandages, water and sponge,
Straight and swift to my wounded I go,
Where they lie on the ground after the battle brought in,
Where their priceless blood reddens the grass, the ground,
Or to the rows of the hospital tent, or under the roof'd hospital,
To the long rows of cots up and down each side I return,
To each and all one after another I draw near, not one do I miss,
An attendant follows holding a tray, he carries a refuse pail,
Soon to be fill'd with clotted rags and blood, emptied, and fill'd
    again.

I onward go, I stop,
With hinged knees and steady hand to dress wounds,
I am firm with each, the pangs are sharp yet unavoidable,
One turns to me his appealing eyes – poor boy! I never knew
    you,
Yet I think I could not refuse this moment to die for you, if that
    would save you.

III

On, on I go, (open doors of time! open hospital doors!)
The crush'd head I dress (poor crazed hand tear not the
    bandage away),

The neck of the cavalry-man with the bullet through and
    through I examine,
Hard the breathing rattles, quite glazed already the eye, yet life
    struggles hard
(Come sweet death! be persuaded O beautiful death!
In mercy come quickly).

From the stump of the arm, the amputated hand,
I undo the clotted lint, remove the slough, wash off the matter
    and blood,
Back on his pillow the soldier bends with curv'd neck and side-
    falling head,
His eyes are closed, his face is pale, he dares not look on the
    bloody stump,
And has not yet look'd on it.

I dress a wound in the side, deep, deep,
But a day or two more, for see the frame all wasted and
    sinking,
And the yellow-blue countenance see.
I dress the perforated shoulder, the foot with the bullet-wound,
Cleanse the one with a gnawing and putrid gangrene, so
    sickening, so offensive,

While the attendant stands behind aside me holding the tray
  and pail.

I am faithful, I do not give out,
The fractur'd thigh, the knee, the wound in the abdomen,
These and more I dress with impassive hand (yet deep in my
  breast a fire, a burning flame).

IV

Thus in silence in dreams' projections,
Returning, resuming, I thread my way through the hospitals,
The hurt and wounded I pacify with soothing hand,
I sit by the restless all the dark night, some are so young,
Some suffer so much, I recall the experience sweet and sad,
(Many a soldier's loving arms about this neck have cross'd and
  rested,
Many a soldier's kiss dwells on these bearded lips).

Walt Whitman

ON THE IDLE HILL OF SUMMER

On the idle hill of summer,
      Sleepy with the flow of streams,
Far I hear the steady drummer
      Drumming like a noise in dreams.

Far and near and low and louder
      On the roads of earth go by,
Dear to friends and food for powder,
      Soldiers marching, all to die.

East and west on fields forgotten
      Bleach the bones of comrades slain,
Lovely lads and dead and rotten;
      None that go return again.

Far the calling bugles hollo,
      High the screaming fife replies,
Gay the files of scarlet follow:
      Woman bore me, I will rise.

A. E. Housman

LANCER

I 'listed at home for a lancer,
> *Oh who would not sleep with the brave?*
I 'listed at home for a lancer
> To ride on a horse to my grave.

And over the seas we were bidden
> A country to take and to keep;
And far with the brave I have ridden,
> And now with the brave I shall sleep.

For round me the men will be lying
> That learned me the way to behave,
And showed me my business of dying:
> *Oh who would not sleep with the brave?*

They ask, and there is not an answer;
Says I, I will 'list for a lancer,
> *Oh who would not sleep with the brave?*

And I with the brave shall be sleeping
> At ease on my mattress of loam,
When back from their taking and keeping
> The squadron is riding at home.

The wind with the plumes will be playing,
    The girls will stand watching them wave,
And eyeing my comrades and saying
    Oh who would not sleep with the brave?

They ask, and there is not an answer;
Says you, I will 'list for a lancer,
    Oh who would not sleep with the brave?

A. E. Housman

* * *

WAR

I

A tent that is pitched at the base:
    A wagon that copies from the night:
A stretcher – and on it a Case:
    A surgeon, who's holding a light.
The Infantry's bearing the brunt –
    O hark to the wind-carried cheer!
A mutter of guns at the front:
    A whimper of sobs at the rear.
And it's *War*! 'Orderly, hold the light.

You can lay him down on the table : so.
Easily – gently! Thanks – you may go.'
    And it's *War*! but the part that is not for show.

II

A tent, with a table athwart,
    A table that's laid out for one;
A waterproof cover – and nought
    But the limp, mangled work of a gun.
A bottle that's stuck by the pole,
    A guttering dip in its neck;
The flickering light of a soul
    On the wondering eyes of The Wreck,
And it's *War*! 'Orderly, hold his hand.
    I'm not going to hurt you, so don't be afraid.
A ricochet! God! what a mess it has made!'
    And it's *War*! and a very unhealthy trade.

III

The clink of a stopper and glass:
    A sigh as the chloroform drips:
A trickle of – what? on the grass.
    And bluer and bluer the lips.
The lashes have hidden the stare…

A rent and the clothes fall away...
A touch, and the wound is laid bare...
A cut, and the face has turned grey...
And it's *War*! 'Orderly, take It out.
It's hard for his child, and it's rough on his wife,
There might have been – sooner – a chance for his life.
But it's *War*! And Orderly, clean this knife!'

Edgar Wallace

* * *

ANTHEM FOR DOOMED YOUTH

What passing-bells for these who die as cattle?
Only the monstrous anger of the guns.
Only the stuttering rifles' rapid rattle
Can patter out their hasty orisons.
No mockeries now for them; no prayers nor bells,
Nor any voice of mourning save the choirs, –
The shrill, demented choirs of wailing shells;
And bugles calling for them from sad shires.

What candles may be held to speed them all?
Not in the hands of boys, but in their eyes

Shall shine the holy glimmers of goodbyes.
      The pallor of girls' brows shall be their pall;
Their flowers the tenderness of patient minds,
And each slow dusk a drawing-down of blinds.

Wilfred Owen

* * *

AUGUST 1914

What in our lives is burnt
In the fire of this?
The heart's dear granary?
The much we shall miss?

Three lives hath one life –
Iron, honey, gold.
The gold, the honey gone –
Left is the hard and cold.

Iron are our lives
Molten right through our youth.
A burnt space through ripe fields,
A fair mouth's broken tooth.

Isaac Rosenberg

THE SILENT ONE

Who died on the wires, and hung there, one of two –
Who for his hours of life had chattered through
Infinite lovely chatter of Bucks accent:
Yet faced unbroken wires; stepped over, and went
A noble fool, faithful to his stripes – and ended.
But I weak, hungry, and willing only for the chance
Of line – to fight in the line, lay down under unbroken
Wires, and saw the flashes and kept unshaken,
Till the politest voice – a finicking accent, said:
'Do you think you might crawl through there: there's a hole.'
Darkness shot at: I smiled, as politely replied –
'I'm afraid not, Sir.' There was no hole, no way to be seen
Nothing but chance of death, after tearing of clothes.
Kept flat, and watched the darkness, hearing bullets whizzing –
And thought of music – and swore deep heart's oaths
(Polite to God) and retreated and came on again,
Again retreated a second time, faced the screen.

Ivor Gurney

ALL THE HILLS AND VALES ALONG

All the hills and vales along
Earth is bursting into song,
And the singers are the chaps
Who are going to die perhaps.
   O sing, marching men,
   Till the valleys ring again.
   Give your gladness to earth's keeping,
   So be glad, when you are sleeping.

Cast away regret and rue,
Think what you are marching to.
Little live, great pass.
Jesus Christ and Barabbas
Were found the same day.
This died, that went his way.
   So sing with joyful breath.
   For why, you are going to death.
   Teeming earth will surely store
   All the gladness that you pour.

Earth that never doubts nor fears,
Earth that knows of death, not tears,
Earth that bore with joyful ease
Hemlock for Socrates,
Earth that blossomed and was glad
'Neath the cross that Christ had,
Shall rejoice and blossom too
When the bullet reaches you.
    Wherefore, men marching
    On the road to death, sing!
    Pour your gladness on earth's head,
    So be merry, so be dead.

From the hills and valleys earth
Shouts back the sound of mirth,
Tramp of feet and lilt of song
Ringing all the road along.
All the music of their going,
Ringing, swinging, glad song-throwing,
Earth will echo still, when foot
Lies numb and voice mute.
    On, marching men, on
    To the gates of death with song.

Sow your gladness for earth's reaping,
So you may be glad, though sleeping.
Strew your gladness on earth's bed,
So be merry, so be dead.

Charles Hamilton Sorley

* * *

APOLOGIA PRO POEMATE MEO

I, too, saw God through mud –
The mud that cracked on cheeks when wretches smiled.
War brought more glory to their eyes than blood,
And gave their laughs more glee than shakes a child.

Merry it was to laugh there –
Where death becomes absurd and life absurder.
For power was on us as we slashed bones bare
Not to feel sickness or remorse of murder.

I, too, have dropped off fear –
Behind the barrage, dead as my platoon,
And sailed my spirit surging, light and clear,
Past the entanglement where hopes lie strewn;

And witnessed exhultation –
Faces that used to curse me, scowl for scowl,
Shine and lift up with passion of oblation,
Seraphic for an hour, though they were foul.

I have made fellowships –
Untold of happy lovers in old song.
For love is not the binding of fair lips
With the soft silk of eyes that look and long.

By joy, whose ribbon slips, –
But wound with war's hard wire whose stakes are strong;
Bound with the bandage of the arm that drips;
Knit in the webbing of the rifle-thong.

I have perceived much beauty
In the hoarse oaths that kept our courage straight;
Heard music in the silentness of duty;
Found peace where shell-storms spouted reddest spate.

Nevertheless, except you share
With them in hell the sorrowful dark of hell,
Whose world is but a trembling of a flare
And heaven but a highway for a shell,

You shall not hear their mirth:
You shall not come to think them well content
By any jest of mine. These men are worth
Your tears: You are not worth their merriment.

Wilfred Owen

* * *

AS THE TEAM'S HEAD-BRASS

As the team's head-brass flashed out on the turn
The lovers disappeared into the wood.
I sat among the boughs of the fallen elm
That strewed the angle of the fallow, and
Watched the plough narrowing a yellow square
Of charlock. Every time the horses turned
Instead of treading me down, the ploughman leaned
Upon the handles to say or ask a word,
About the weather, next about the war.
Scraping the share he faced towards the wood,
And screwed along the furrow till the brass flashed
Once more.
      The blizzard felled the elm whose crest
I sat in, by a woodpecker's round hole,

The ploughman said, 'When will they take it away?'
'When the war's over.' So the talk began –
One minute and an interval of ten,
A minute more and the same interval.
'Have you been out?' 'No.' 'And don't want to, perhaps?'
'If I could only come back again, I should.
I could spare an arm, I shouldn't want to lose
A leg. If I should lose my head, why, so,
I should want nothing more… Have many gone
From here?' 'Yes.' 'Many lost?' 'Yes, a good few.
Only two teams work on the farm this year.
One of my mates is dead. The second day
In France they killed him. It was back in March,
The very night of the blizzard, too. Now if
He had stayed here we should have moved the tree.'
'And I should not have sat here. Everything
Would have been different. For it would have been
Another world.' 'Ay, and a better, though
If we could see all all might seem good.' Then
The lovers came out of the wood again:
The horses started and for the last time
I watched the clods crumble and topple over
After the ploughshare and the stumbling team.

Edward Thomas

Returning, We Hear the Larks

Sombre the night is.
And though we have our lives, we know
What sinister threat lurks there.

Dragging these anguished limbs, we only know
This poison-blasted track opens on our camp –
On a little safe sleep.

But hark! joy – joy – strange joy.
Lo! heights of night ringing with unseen larks.
Music showering on our upturned list'ning faces.

Death could drop from the dark
As easily as song –
But song only dropped,
Like a blind man's dreams on the sand
By dangerous tides,
Like a girl's dark hair for she dreams no ruin lies there,
Or her kisses where a serpent hides.

Isaac Rosenberg

INSENSIBILITY

I

Happy are men who yet before they are killed
Can let their veins run cold.
Whom no compassion fleers
Or makes their feet
Sore on the alleys cobbled with their brothers.
The front line withers,
But they are troops who fade, not flowers
For poets' tearful fooling:
Men, gaps for filling
Losses who might have fought
Longer; but no one bothers.

II

And some cease feeling
Even themselves or for themselves.
Dullness best solves
The tease and doubt of shelling,
And Chance's strange arithmetic
Comes simpler than the reckoning of their shilling.
They keep no check on Armies' decimation.

III

Happy are these who lose imagination:

They have enough to carry with ammunition.

Their spirit drags no pack.

Their old wounds save with cold cannot more ache.

Having seen all things red,

Their eyes are rid

Of the hurt of the colour of blood for ever.

And terror's first constriction over,

Their hearts remain small drawn.

Their senses in some scorching cautery of battle

Now long since ironed,

Can laugh among the dying, unconcerned.

IV

Happy the soldier home, with not a notion

How somewhere, every dawn, some men attack,

And many sighs are drained.

Happy the lad whose mind was never trained:

His days are worth forgetting more than not.

He sings along the march

Which we march taciturn, because of dusk,

The long, forlorn, relentless trend

From larger day to huger night.

V

We wise, who with a thought besmirch
Blood over all our soul,
How should we see our task
But through his blunt and lashless eyes?
Alive, he is not vital overmuch;
Dying, not mortal overmuch;
Nor sad, nor proud,
Nor curious at all.
He cannot tell
Old men's placidity from his.

VI

But cursed are dullards whom no cannon stuns,
That they should be as stones.
Wretched are they, and mean
With paucity that never was simplicity.
By choice they made themselves immune
To pity and whatever mourns in man
Before the last sea and the hapless stars;
Whatever mourns when many leave these shores;
Whatever shares
The eternal reciprocity of tears.

Wilfred Owen

THE NIGHT PATROL

Over the top! The wire's thin here, unbarbed
Plain rusty coils, not staked, and low enough:
Full of old tins, though – 'When you're through, all three,
Aim quarter left for fifty yards or so,
Then straight for that new piece of German wire;
See if it's thick, and listen for a while
For sounds of working; don't run any risks;
About an hour; now, over!'

                    And we placed
Our hands on the topmost sand-bags, leapt, and stood
A second with curved backs, then crept to the wire,
Wormed ourselves tinkling through, glanced back, and
   dropped.
The sodden ground was splashed with shallow pools,
And tufts of crackling cornstalks, two years old,
No man had reaped, and patches of spring grass,
Half-seen, as rose and sank the flares, were strewn
The wrecks of our attack: the bandoliers,
Packs, rifles, bayonets, belts, and haversacks,
Shell fragments, and the huge whole forms of shells
Shot fruitlessly – and everywhere the dead.
Only the dead were always present – present

As a vile sickly smell of rottenness;
The rustling stubble and the early grass,
The slimy pools – the dead men stank through all,
Pungent and sharp; as bodies loomed before,
And as we passed, they stank: then dulled away
To that vague fœtor, all encompassing,
Infecting earth and air. They lay, all clothed,
Each in some new and piteous attitude
That we well marked to guide us back: as he,
Outside our wire, that lay on his back and crossed
His legs Crusader-wise; I smiled at that,
And thought on Elia and his Temple Church.
From him, at quarter left, lay a small corpse,
Down in a hollow, huddled as in a bed,
That one of us put his hand on unawares.
Next was a bunch of half a dozen men
All blown to bits, an archipelago
Of corrupt fragments, vexing to us three,
Who had no light to see by, save the flares.
On such a trail, so lit, for ninety yards
We crawled on belly and elbows, till we saw,
Instead of lumpish dead before our eyes,
The stakes and crosslines of the German wire.

We lay in shelter of the last dead man,
Ourselves as dead, and heard their shovels ring
Turning the earth, then talk and cough at times.
A sentry fired and a machine-gun spat;
They shot a glare above us, when it fell
And spluttered out in the pools of No Man's Land,
We turned and crawled past the remembered dead:
Past him and him, and them and him, until,
For he lay some way apart, we caught the scent
Of the Crusader and slid past his legs,
And through the wire and home, and got our rum.

Arthur Graeme West

* * *

DULCE ET DECORUM EST

Bent double, like old beggars under sacks,
Knock-kneed, coughing like hags, we cursed through sludge,
Till on the haunting flares we turned our backs
And towards our distant rest began to trudge.
Men marched asleep. Many had lost their boots
But limped on, blood-shod. All went lame; all blind;
Drunk with fatigue; deaf even to the hoots

Of tired, outstripped Five-Nines that dropped behind.
Gas! GAS! Quick, boys! An ecstasy of fumbling,
Fitting the clumsy helmets just in time;
But someone still was yelling out and stumbling,
And flound'ring like a man in fire or lime
Dim, through the misty panes and thick green light,
As under a green sea, I saw him drowning.

In all my dreams, before my helpless sight,
He plunges at me, guttering, choking, drowning.

If in some smothering dreams you too could pace
Behind the wagon that we flung him in,
And watch the white eyes writhing in his face,
His hanging face, like a devil's sick of sin;
If you could hear, at every jolt, the blood
Come gargling from the froth-corrupted lungs,
Obscene as cancer, bitter as the cud
Of vile, incurable sores on innocent tongues, –
My friend, you would not tell with such high zest
To children ardent for some desperate glory,
The old Lie; *Dulce et Decorum est*
Pro patria mori.

Wilfred Owen

Eyes of men running, falling, screaming

Eyes of men running, falling, screaming
Eyes of men shouting, sweating, bleeding
The eyes of the fearful, those of the sad
The eyes of exhaustion, and those of the mad.

Eyes of men thinking, hoping, waiting
Eyes of men loving, cursing, hating
The eyes of the wounded, sodden in red
The eyes of the dying and those of the dead.

Anonymous

Last Song

All my songs are risen and fled away;
(Only the brave birds stay);
All my beautiful songs are broken or fled.
My poor songs could not stay
Among the filth and the weariness and the dead.

There was bloody grime on their light, white
    feathery wings,
(Hear how the lark still sings),
And their eyes were the eyes of dead men that I knew.
Only a madman sings
When half of his friends lie asleep for the rain and
    the dew.

The flowers will grow over the bones of my friends;
(The birds' song never ends);
Winter and summer, their fair flesh turns to clay.
Perhaps before all ends
My songs will come again that have fled away.

Henry Lamont Simpson

Here, Bullet

Mosul, Iraq, February 2004

If a body is what you want,
then here is bone and gristle and flesh.
Here is the clavicle-snapped wish,
the aorta's opened valves, the leap
thought makes at the synaptic gap.
Here is the adrenaline rush you crave,
that inexorable flight, that insane puncture
into heat and blood. And I dare you to finish
what you've started. Because here, Bullet,
here is where I complete the word you bring
hissing through the air, here is where I moan
the barrel's cold esophagus, triggering
my tongue's explosives for the rifling I have
inside of me, each twist of the round
spun deeper, because here, Bullet,
here is where the world ends, every time.

Brian Turner

PREMONITIONS

I have a rendezvous with Death

At some disputed barricade,

When Spring comes back with rustling shade

And apple-blossoms fill the air –

I have a rendezvous with Death

When Spring brings back blue days and fair…

A Burnt Ship

Out of a fired ship, which by no way
But drowning could be rescued from the flame,
Some men leap'd forth, and ever as they came
Near the foes' ships, did by their shot decay;
So all were lost, which in the ship were found,
    They in the sea being burnt, they in the burnt
      ship drowned.

John Donne

* * *

Drummer Hodge

I

They throw in Drummer Hodge, to rest
    Uncoffined – just as found:
His landmark is a kopje-crest
    That breaks the veldt around;
And foreign constellations west
    Each night above his mound.

II

Young Hodge the Drummer never knew –
Fresh from his Wessex home –
The meaning of the broad Karoo,
The Bush, the dusty loam,
And why uprose to nightly view
Strange stars amid the gloam.

III

Yet portion of that unknown plain
Will Hodge forever be;
His homely Northern breast and brain
Grow to some Southern tree,
And strange-eyed constellation reign
His stars eternally.

Thomas Hardy

* * *

DANNY DEEVER

'What are the bugles blowin' for?' said Files-on-Parade.
'To turn you out, to turn you out,' the Colour-Sergeant said.
'What makes you look so white, so white?' said Files-on-Parade.

'I'm dreadin' what I've got to watch,' the Colour-Sergeant said.
> For they're hangin' Danny Deever, you can hear the Dead
> March play,
> The regiment's in 'ollow square – they're hangin' him today;
> They've taken of his buttons off an' cut his stripes away,
> An' they're hangin' Danny Deever in the mornin'.

'What makes the rear-rank breathe so 'ard?' said Files-on-Parade.
'It's bitter cold, it's bitter cold,' the Colour-Sergeant said.
'What makes that front-rank man fall down?' said Files-on-
  Parade.
'A touch o' sun, a touch o' sun', the Colour-Sergeant said.
> They are hangin' Danny Deever, they are marchin' of 'im
> round,
> They 'ave 'alted Danny Deever by 'is coffin on the ground;
> An' 'e'll swing in 'arf a minute for a sneakin' shootin'
> hound –
> O they're hangin' Danny Deever in the mornin'!

''Is cot was right-'and cot to mine,' said Files-on-Parade.
''E's sleepin' out an' far tonight,' the Colour-Sergeant said.
'I've drunk 'is beer a score o' times,' said Files-on-Parade.
''E's drinkin' bitter beer alone,' the Colour-Sergeant said.
> They are hangin' Danny Deever, you must mark 'im to 'is
> place,

For 'e shot a comrade sleepin' – you must look 'im in the face;
Nine 'undred of 'is county an' the regiment's disgrace,
While they're hangin' Danny Deever in the mornin'.

'What's that so black agin' the sun?' said Files-on-Parade.
'It's Danny fightin' 'ard for life,' the Colour-Sergeant said.
'What's that that whimpers over'ead?' said Files-on-Parade.
'It's Danny's soul that's passin' now,' the Colour-Sergeant said.
For they're done with Danny Deever, you can 'ear the
quickstep play,
The regiment's in column, an' they're marchin' us away;
Ho! the young recruits are shakin', an' they'll want their
beer today,
After hangin' Danny Deever in the mornin'.

Rudyard Kipling

* * *

GRENADIER

The Queen she sent to look for me,
The sergeant he did say,
'Young man, a soldier will you be
For thirteen pence a day?'

For thirteen pence a day did I
      Take off the things I wore,
And I have marched to where I lie,
      And I shall march no more.

My mouth is dry, my shirt is wet,
      My blood runs all away,
So now I shall not die in debt
      For thirteen pence a day.

Tomorrow after new young men
      The sergeant he must see,
For things will all be over then
      Between the Queen and me.

And I shall have to bate my price,
      For in the grave, they say,
Is neither knowledge nor device
      Nor thirteen pence a day.

A. E. Housman

He Fell among Thieves

'Ye have robb'd,' said he, 'ye have slaughter'd and made an end,
　　　Take your ill-got plunder, and bury the dead:
What will ye more of your guest and sometime friend?'
　　　'Blood for our blood,' they said.

He laugh'd: 'If one may settle the score for five,
　　　I am ready; but let the reckoning stand till day:
I have loved the sunlight as dearly as any alive.'
　　　'You shall die at dawn,' said they.

He flung his empty revolver down the slope,
　　　He climb'd alone to the Eastward edge of the trees;
All night long in a dream untroubled of hope
　　　He brooded, clasping his knees.

He did not hear the monotonous roar that fills
　　　The ravine where the Yassîn river sullenly flows;
He did not see the starlight on the Laspur hills,
　　　Or the far Afghan snows.

He saw the April noon on his books aglow,
　　　The wistaria trailing in at the window wide;

He heard his father's voice from the terrace below
        Calling him down to ride.

He saw the gray little church across the park,
        The mounds that hid the loved and honour'd dead;
The Norman arch, the chancel softly dark,
        The brasses black and red.

He saw the School Close, sunny and green,
        The runner beside him, the stand by the parapet wall,
The distant tape, and the crowd roaring between,
        His own name over all.

He saw the dark wainscot and timber'd roof,
        The long tables, and the faces merry and keen;
The College Eight and their trainer dining aloof,
        The Dons on the daïs serene.

He watch'd the liner's stem ploughing the foam,
        He felt her trembling speed and the thrash of her screw;
He heard the passengers' voices talking of home,
        He saw the flag she flew.

And now it was dawn. He rose strong on his feet,
        And strode to his ruin'd camp below the wood;

He drank the breath of the morning cool and sweet:
　　　His murderers round him stood.

Light on the Laspur hills was broadening fast,
　　　　The blood-red snow-peaks chill'd to a dazzling
　　　　　　white;
He turn'd, and saw the golden circle at last,
　　　Cut by the Eastern height.

'O glorious Life, Who dwellest in earth and sun,
　　　I have lived, I praise and adore Thee.'
　　　　A sword swept.
Over the pass the voices one by one
　　　Faded, and the hill slept.

Sir Henry Newbolt

* * *

SLAIN

Dulce et decorum est pro patria mori

You who are still and white
And cold like stone;

For whom the unfailing light
Is spent and done;

For whom no more the breath
Of dawn, nor evenfall,
Nor Spring nor love or death
Matter at all;

Who were so strong and young,
And brave and wise,
And on the dark are flung
With darkened eyes;

Who roystered and caroused
But yesterday,
And now are dumbly housed
In stranger clay;

Who valiantly led,
Who followed valiantly,
Who knew no touch of dread
Of that which was to be;

Children that were nought
Ere ye were tried,

How have ye dared and fought,
    Triumphed and died!

Yea, it is very sweet
    And decorous
The omnipotent Shade to meet
    And flatter thus.

T. W. H. Crosland

* * *

THE UNCONQUERED DEAD

' . . . defeated, with great loss.'

Not we the conquered! Not to us the blame
    Of them that flee, of them that basely yield;
Nor ours the shout of victory, the fame
    Of them that vanquish in a stricken field.

That day of battle in the dusty heat
    We lay and heard the bullets swish and sing
Like scythes amid the over-ripened wheat,
    And we the harvest of their garnering.

Some yielded, No, not we! Not we, we swear
    By these our wounds; this trench upon the hill
Where all the shell-strewn earth is seamed and bare,
    Was ours to keep; and lo! we have it still.

We might have yielded, even we, but death
    Came for our helper; like a sudden flood
The crashing darkness fell; our painful breath
    We drew with gasps amid the choking blood.

The roar fell faint and farther off, and soon
    Sank to a foolish humming in our ears,
Like crickets in the long, hot afternoon
    Among the wheat fields of the olden years.

Before our eyes a boundless wall of red
    Shot through by sudden streaks of jagged pain!
Then a slow-gathering darkness overhead
    And rest came on us like a quiet rain.

Not we the conquered! Not to us the shame,
    Who hold our earthen ramparts, nor shall cease
To hold them ever; victors we, who came
    In that fierce moment to our honoured peace.

John McCrae

Epitaph on an Army of Mercenaries

These, in the day when heaven was falling,
    The hour when earth's foundations fled,
Followed their mercenary calling
    And took their wages and are dead.

Their shoulders held the sky suspended;
    They stood, and earth's foundations stay;
What God abandoned, these defended,
    And saved the sum of things for pay.

A. E. Housman

* * *

In Memoriam (Easter, 1915)

The flowers left thick at nightfall in the wood
This Eastertide call into mind the men,
Now far from home, who, with their sweethearts, should
Have gathered them and will do never again.

Edward Thomas

THE BALLAD OF THE THREE SPECTRES

As I went up by Ovillers
        In mud and water cold to the knee,
There went three jeering, fleeing spectres,
        That walked abreast and talked of me.

The first said, 'Here's a right brave soldier
        That walks the dark unfearingly;
Soon he'll come back on a fine stretcher,
        And laughing for a nice Blighty.'

The second, 'Read his face, old comrade,
        No kind of lucky chance I see;
One day he'll freeze in mud to the marrow,
        Then look his last on Picardie.'

Though bitter the word of these first twain
        Curses the third spat venomously;
'He'll stay untouched till the war's last dawning
        Then live one hour of agony.'

Liars the first two were. Behold me
    At sloping arms by one – two – three;
Waiting the time I shall discover
    Whether the third spake verity.

Ivor Gurney

* * *

THE ANXIOUS DEAD

O guns, fall silent till the dead men hear
    Above their heads the legions pressing on:
(These fought their fight in time of bitter fear,
    And died not knowing how the day had gone.)

O flashing muzzles, pause, and let them see
    The coming dawn that streaks the sky afar;
Then let your mighty chorus witness be
    To them, and Caesar, that we still make war.

Tell them, O guns, that we have heard their call,
    That we have sworn, and will not turn aside,
That we will onward till we win or fall,
    That we will keep the faith for which they died.

Bid them be patient, and some day, anon,
        They shall feel earth enwrapt in silence deep;
Shall greet, in wonderment, the quiet dawn,
        And in content may turn them to their sleep.

John McCrae

* * *

HERE DEAD WE LIE

Here dead we lie
Because we did not choose
To live and shame the land
From which we sprung.

Life, to be sure,
Is nothing much to lose,
But young men think it is,
And we were young.

A. E. Housman

THE MAN HE KILLED

Had he and I but met
      By some old ancient inn,
We should have set us down to wet
      Right many a nipperkin!

      But ranged as infantry,
      And staring face to face,
I shot at him as he at me,
      And killed him in his place.

      I shot him dead because –
      Because he was my foe,
Just so: my foe of course he was;
      That's clear enough; although

      He thought he'd 'list, perhaps,
      Off-hand like – just as I –
Was out of work – had sold his traps –
      No other reason why.

Yes; quaint and curious war is!
You shoot a fellow down
You'd treat, if met where any bar is,
Or help to half a crown.

Thomas Hardy

* * *

THE SHELL HOLE

In the Shell Hole he lies, this German soldier of a year ago;
But he is not as then, accoutred, well, and eager for the foe
He hoped so soon, so utterly, to crush. His muddy skull
Lies near the mangled remnants of his corpse – war's furies thus
   annul
The pomp and pageantry that were its own. White rigid bones
Gape through the nauseous chaos of his clothes; the cruel stones
Hold fast the letter he was wont to clasp close to his am'rous
   breast.
Here 'neath the stark, keen stars, where is no peace, no joy, nor
   any rest,
He lies. There, to the right, his boot, gashed by the great shell's
   fiendish whim,

Retains – O horrid spectacle! – the fleshless stump that was his
    limb!
Vile rats and mice, and flies and lice and ghastly things that
    carrion know
Have made a travesty of Death of him who lived a year ago.

Hamish Mann

* * *

STRANGE MEETING

It seemed that out of the battle I escaped
Down some profound dull tunnel, long since scooped
Through granites which Titanic wars had groined.
Yet also there encumbered sleepers groaned,
Too fast in thought or death to be bestirred.
Then, as I probed them, one sprang up, and stared
With piteous recognition in fixed eyes,
Lifting distressful hands as if to bless.
And by his smile, I knew that sullen hall;
By his dead smile I knew we stood in Hell.
With a thousand fears that vision's face was grained;
Yet no blood reached there from the upper ground,
And no guns thumped, or down the flues made moan.

'Strange, friend,' I said, 'Here is no cause to mourn.'
'None,' said the other, 'Save the undone years,
The hopelessness. Whatever hope is yours,
Was my life also; I went hunting wild
After the wildest beauty in the world,
Which lies not calm in eyes, or braided hair,
But mocks the steady running of the hour,
And if it grieves, grieves richlier than here.
For by my glee might many men have laughed,
And of my weeping something has been left,
Which must die now. I mean the truth untold,
The pity of war, the pity war distilled.
Now men will go content with what we spoiled.
Or, discontent, boil bloody, and be spilled.
They will be swift with swiftness of the tigress,
None will break ranks, though nations trek from progress.
Courage was mine, and I had mystery;
Wisdom was mine, and I had mastery;
To miss the march of this retreating world
Into vain citadels that are not walled.
Then, when much blood had clogged their chariot-wheels
I would go up and wash them from sweet wells,
Even with truths that lie too deep for taint.

I would have poured my spirit without stint
But not through wounds; not on the cess of war.
Foreheads of men have bled where no wounds were.
I am the enemy you killed, my friend.
I knew you in this dark; for so you frowned
Yesterday through me as you jabbed and killed.
I parried; but my hands were loath and cold.
Let us sleep now . . . '

Wilfred Owen

* * *

I HAVE A RENDEZVOUS WITH DEATH

I have a rendezvous with Death
At some disputed barricade,
When Spring comes back with rustling shade
And apple-blossoms fill the air –
I have a rendezvous with Death
When Spring brings back blue days and fair.

It may be he shall take my hand
And lead me into his dark land

And close my eyes and quench my breath –
It may be I shall pass him still.
I have a rendezvous with Death
On some scarred slope of battered hill,
When Spring comes round again this year
And the first meadow-flowers appear.

God knows't were better to be deep
Pillowed in silk and scented down,
Where Love throbs out in blissful sleep
Pulse nigh to pulse, and breath to breath,
Where hushed awakenings are dear . . .
But I've a rendezvous with Death
At midnight in some flaming town,
When Spring trips north again this year,
And I to my pledged word am true,
I shall not fail that rendezvous.

Alan Seeger

THE BOHEMIANS

Certain people would not clean their buttons,
Nor polish buckles after latest fashions,
Preferred their hair long, putties comfortable,
Barely escaping hanging, indeed hardly able;
In Bridge and smoking without army cautions
Spending hours that sped like evil for quickness,
(While others burnished brasses, earned promotions)
These were those ones who jested in the trench,
While others argued of army ways, and wrenched
What little soul they had still further from shape,
And died off one by one, or became officers,
Without the first of dream, the ghost of notions
Of ever becoming soldiers, or smart and neat,
Surprised as ever to find the army capable
Of sounding 'Lights out' to break a game of Bridge,
As to fear candles would set a barn alight:
In Artois or Picardy they lie – free of useless fashions.

Ivor Gurney

An Irish Airman Foresees His Death

Know that I shall meet my fate
Somewhere among the clouds above;
Those that I fight I do not hate
Those that I guard I do not love;
My country is Kiltartan Cross,
My countrymen Kiltartan's poor,
No likely end could bring them loss
Or leave them happier than before.
Nor law, nor duty bade me fight,
Nor public man, nor cheering crowds,
A lonely impulse of delight
Drove to this tumult in the clouds;
I balanced all, brought all to mind,
The years to come seemed waste of breath,
A waste of breath the years behind
In balance with this life, this death.

W. B. Yeats

WHEN YOU SEE MILLIONS OF THE MOUTHLESS DEAD

When you see millions of the mouthless dead
Across your dreams in pale battalions go,
Say not soft things as other men have said,
That you'll remember. For you need not so.
Give them not praise. For, deaf, how should they know
It is not curses heaped on each gashed head?
Nor tears. Their blind eyes see not your tears flow.
Nor honour. It is easy to be dead.
Say only this, 'They are dead.' Then add thereto,
'Yet many a better one has died before.'
Then, scanning all the overcrowded mass, should you
Perceive one face that you loved heretofore,
It is a spook. None wears the face you knew.
Great death has made all this for evermore.

Charles Hamilton Sorley

THE SOLDIER

'Tis strange to look on a man that is dead
As he lies in the shell-swept hell
And to think that the poor black battered corpse
Once lived like you and was well.

'Tis stranger far when you come to think
That you may soon be like him…
And it's Fear that tugs at your trembling soul,
A Fear that is weird and grim!

Hamish Mann

* * *

THE CHERRY TREES

The cherry trees bend over and are shedding
On the old road where all that passed are dead,
Their petals, stewing the grass as for a wedding
This early May morn when there is none to wed.

Edward Thomas

TO MARGOT HEINEMANN

Heart of the heartless world,
Dear heart, the thought of you
Is the pain at my side,
The shadow that chills my view.

The wind rises in the evening,
Reminds that autumn's near.
I am afraid to lose you,
I am afraid of my fear.

On the last mile to Huesca,
The last fence for our pride,
Think so kindly, dear, that I
Sense you at my side.

And if bad luck should lay my strength
Into the shallow grave,
Remember all the good you can;
Don't forget my love.

John Cornford

Vergissmeinnicht

Three weeks gone and the combatants gone
returning over the nightmare ground
we found the place again, and found
the soldier sprawling in the sun.

The frowning barrel of his gun
overshadowing. As we came on
that day, he hit my tank with one
like the entry of a demon.

Look. Here in the gunpit spoil
the dishonoured picture of his girl
who has put: Steffi. Vergissmeinnicht.
in a copybook gothic script.

We see him almost with content,
abased, and seeming to have paid
and mocked at by his own equipment
that's hard and good when he's decayed.

But she would weep to see today
how on his skin the swart flies move;
the dust upon the paper eye
and the burst stomach like a cave.

For here the lover and killer are mingled
who had one body and one heart.
And death who had the soldier singled
has done the lover mortal hurt.

Keith Douglas

* * *

THE DEAD AT QUANG TRI

This is harder than counting stones
along paths going nowhere, the way
a tiger circles & backtracks by
smelling his blood on the ground.
The one kneeling beside the pagoda,
remember him? Captain, we won't

talk about that. The Buddhist boy
at the gate with the shaven head
we rubbed for good luck
glides by like a white moon.
He won't stay dead, dammit!
Blades aim for the family jewels;
the grass we walk on
won't stay down.

Yusef Komunyakaa

SPIRIT AND FAITH

Now, God be thanked Who has matched us with His hour,

　　And caught our youth, and wakened us from sleeping,

With hand made sure, clear eye, and sharpened power,

　　To turn, as swimmers into cleanness leaping,

Glad from a world grown old and cold and weary...

RULE, BRITANNIA

When Britain first at Heaven's command
  Arose from out the azure main,
This was the charter of her land,
  And guardian angels sung the strain:
Rule, Britannia! rule the waves!
  Britons never will be slaves!

The nations not so blest as thee
  Must in their turn to tyrants fall,
Whilst thou shalt flourish great and free
  The dread and envy of them all.

Still more majestic shalt thou rise,
  More dreadful from each foreign stroke;
As the loud blast that tears the skies
  Serves but to root thy native oak.

Thee haughty tyrants ne'er shall tame;
  All their attempts to bend thee down
Will but arouse thy generous flame,
  And work their woe and thy renown.

To thee belongs the rural reign;
      Thy cities shall with commerce shine;
All thine shall be the subject main,
      And every shore it circles thine!

The Muses, still with Freedom found,
      Shall to thy happy coast repair;
Blest Isle, with matchless beauty crown'd
      And manly hearts to guard the fair:
Rule, Britannia! rule the waves!
      Britons never will be slaves!

James Thomson

* * *

LINES ON WAR

I murder hate, by field or flood,
Tho' glory's name may screen us;
In wars at hame I'll spend my blood,
Life-giving wars of Venus.
The deities that I adore,
Are social peace and plenty;

I'm better pleas'd to make one more,
Than be the death o' twenty.

Robert Burns

* * *

Ye Mariners of England

Ye Mariners of England
    That guard our native seas!
Whose flag has braved, a thousand years,
    The battle and the breeze!
Your glorious standard launch again
    To match another foe!
And sweep through the deep,
    While the stormy winds do blow!
While the battle rages loud and long,
    And the stormy winds do blow.

The spirits of your fathers
    Shall start from every wave –
For the deck it was their field of fame,
    And Ocean was their grave:
Where Blake and mighty Nelson fell,

Your manly hearts shall glow,
As ye sweep through the deep,
While the stormy winds do blow!
While the battle rages loud and long,
And the stormy winds do blow.

Britannia needs no bulwarks,
No towers along the steep;
Her march is o'er the mountain-waves,
Her home is on the deep.
With thunders from her native oak
She quells the floods below,
As they roar on the shore,
When the stormy winds do blow!
When the battle rages loud and long,
When the stormy winds do blow.

The meteor flag of England
Shall yet terrific burn;
Till danger's troubled night depart,
And the star of peace return.
Then, then, ye ocean-warriors!
Our song and feast shall flow
To the fame of your name,

When the storm has ceased to blow!
When the fiery fight is heard no more,
And the storm has ceased to blow.

Thomas Campbell

* * *

IT IS NOT TO BE THOUGHT OF

It is not to be thought of that the Flood
Of British freedom, which, to the open sea
Of the world's praise, from dark antiquity
Hath flowed, 'with pomp of waters, unwithstood',
Roused though it be full often to a mood
Which spurns the check of salutary bands,
That this most famous Stream in bogs and sands
Should perish; and to evil and to good
Be lost forever. In our halls is hung
Armoury of the invincible Knights of old:
We must be free or die, who speak the tongue
That Shakspeare spake; the faith and morals hold
Which Milton held. – In everything we are sprung
Of Earth's first blood, have titles manifold.

William Wordsworth

TO THE MEN OF KENT

October 1803

Vanguard of Liberty, ye men of Kent,
Ye children of a Soil that doth advance
Her haughty brow against the coast of France,
Now is the time to prove your hardiment!
To France be words of invitation sent!
They from their fields can see the countenance
Of your fierce war, may ken the glittering lance
And hear you shouting forth your brave intent.
Left single, in bold parley, ye, of yore,
Did from the Norman win a gallant wreath;
Confirmed the charters that were yours before; –
No parleying now! In Britain is one breath;
We all are with you now from shore to shore:
Ye men of Kent, 'tis victory or death!

William Wordsworth

ON THIS DAY I COMPLETE MY THIRTY-SIXTH YEAR

'Tis time this heart should be unmoved,
Since others it hath ceased to move:
Yet, though I cannot be beloved,
Still let me love!

My days are in the yellow leaf;
The flowers and fruits of love are gone;
The worm, the canker, and the grief
Are mine alone!

The fire that on my bosom preys
Is lone as some volcanic isle;
No torch is kindled at its blaze –
A funeral pile.

The hope, the fear, the jealous care,
The exalted portion of the pain
And power of love, I cannot share,
But wear the chain.

But 'tis not *thus* – and 'tis not *here* –
Such thoughts should shake my soul nor *now*,

Where glory decks the hero's bier,
    Or binds his brow.

The sword, the banner, and the field,
    Glory and Greece, around me see!
The Spartan, borne upon his shield,
    Was not more free.

Awake! (not Greece – she *is* awake!)
    Awake, my spirit! Think through whom
Thy life-blood tracks its parent lake,
    And then strike home!

Tread those reviving passions down,
    Unworthy manhood! – unto thee
Indifferent should the smile or frown
    Of beauty be.

If thou regrett'st thy youth, *why live?*
    The land of honourable death
Is here – up to the field, and give
    Away thy breath!

Seek out – less often sought than found –
    A soldier's grave, for thee the best;
Then look around, and choose thy ground,
    And take thy rest.

George Gordon, Lord Byron

* * *

BOSTON HYMN

The word of the Lord by night
To the watching Pilgrims came,
As they sat by the seaside,
And filled their hearts with flame.

God said, I am tired of kings,
I suffer them no more;
Up to my ear the morning brings
The outrage of the poor.

Think ye I made this ball
A field of havoc and war,
Where tyrants great and tyrants small
Might harry the weak and poor?

My angel – his name is Freedom –
Choose him to be your king;
He shall cut pathways east and west
And fend you with his wing.

Lo! I uncover the land
Which I hid of old time in the West,
As the sculptor uncovers the statue
When he has wrought his best;

I show Columbia, of the rocks
Which dip their foot in the seas
And soar to the airborne flocks
Of clouds and the boreal fleece.

I will divide my goods;
Call in the wretch and slave:
None shall rule but the humble,
And none but Toil shall have.

I will have never a noble,
No lineage counted great;
Fishers and choppers and ploughmen
Shall constitute a state.

Go, cut down trees in the forest
And trim the straightest boughs;
Cut down trees in the forest
And build me a wooden house.

Call the people together,
The young men and the sires,
The digger in the harvest-field,
Hireling and him that hires;

And here in a pine state-house
They shall choose men to rule
In every needful faculty,
In church and state and school.

Lo, now! if these poor men
Can govern the land and sea
And make just laws below the sun,
As planets faithful be.

And ye shall succor men;
'Tis nobleness to serve;
Help them who cannot help again:
Beware from right to swerve.

I break your bonds and masterships,
And I unchain the slave:
Free be his heart and hand henceforth
As wind and wandering wave.

I cause from every creature
His proper good to flow:
As much as he is and doeth,
So much he shall bestow.

But, lay hands on another
To coin his labor and sweat,
He goes in pawn for his victim
For eternal years in debt.

Today unbind the captive,
So only are ye unbound;
Lift up a people from the dust,
Trump of their rescue, sound!

Pay ransom to the owner
And fill the bag to the brim.
Who is the owner? The slave is owner,
And ever was. Pay him.

O North! give him beauty for rags,
And honor, O South! for his shame;
Nevada! coin thy golden crags
With Freedom's image and name.

Up! and the dusky race
That sat in darkness long, –
Be swift their feet as antelopes,
And as behemoth strong.

Come, East and West and North,
By races, as snowflakes,
And carry my purpose forth,
Which neither halts nor shakes.

My will fulfilled shall be,
For, in daylight or in dark,
My thunderbolt has eyes to see
His way home to the mark.

Ralph Waldo Emerson

LAUS DEO!

It is done!
Clang of bell and roar of gun
Send the tidings up and down.
How the belfries rock and reel!
How the great guns, peal on peal,
Fling the joy from town to town!

Ring, O bells!
Every stroke exulting tells
Of the burial hour of crime.
Loud and long, that all may hear,
Ring for every listening ear
Of Eternity and Time!

Let us kneel:
God's own voice is in that peal,
And this spot is holy ground.
Lord, forgive us! What are we
That our eyes this glory see,
That our ears have heard this sound!

For the Lord
On the whirlwind is abroad;
In the earthquake He has spoken;
He has smitten with His thunder
The iron walls asunder,
And the gates of brass are broken!

Loud and long
Lift the old exulting song;
Sing with Miriam by the sea,
He has cast the mighty down;
Horse and rider sink and drown;
'He hath triumphed gloriously!'

Did we dare,
In our agony of prayer,
Ask for more than He has done?
When was ever His right hand
Over any time or land
Stretched as now beneath the sun?

How they pale,
Ancient myth and song and tale,

In this wonder of our days
    When the cruel rod of war
    Blossoms white with righteous law,
And the wrath of man is praise!

    Blotted out!
    All within and all about
Shall a fresher life begin;
    Freer breathe the universe
    As it rolls its heavy curse
On the dead and buried sin!

    It is done!
    In the circuit of the sun
Shall the sound thereof go forth.
    It shall bid the sad rejoice,
    It shall give the dumb a voice,
It shall belt with joy the earth!

    Ring and swing,
    Bells of joy! On morning's wing
Sound the song of praise abroad!
    With a sound of broken chains

Tell the nations that He reigns,
Who alone is Lord and God!

John Greenleaf Whittier

* * *

Vitaï Lampada

There's a breathless hush in the Close tonight –
    Ten to make and the match to win –
A bumping pitch and a blinding light,
    An hour to play and the last man in.
And it's not for the sake of a ribboned coat,
    Or the selfish hope of a season's fame,
But his Captain's hand on his shoulder smote –
    'Play up! play up! and play the game!'

The sand of the desert is sodden red, –
    Red with the wreck of a square that broke; –
The Gatling's jammed and the colonel dead,
    And the regiment blind with dust and smoke.
The river of death has brimmed his banks,
    And England's far, and Honour a name,
But the voice of schoolboy rallies the ranks,

'Play up! play up! and play the game!'
This is the word that year by year
    While in her place the School is set
Every one of her sons must hear,
    And none that hears it dare forget.
This they all with a joyful mind
    Bear through life like a torch in flame,
And falling fling to the host behind –
    'Play up! play up! and play the game!'

Sir Henry Newbolt

* * *

A Christmas Ghost-Story

South of the Line, inland from far Durban,
A mouldering soldier lies – your countryman.
Awry and doubled up are his gray bones,
And on the breeze his puzzled phantom moans
Nightly to clear Canopus: 'I would know
By whom and when the All-Earth-gladdening Law
Of Peace, brought in by that Man Crucified,
Was ruled to be inept, and set aside?

And what of logic or of truth appears
In tacking "Anno Domini" to the years?
Near twenty-hundred livened thus have hied,
But tarries yet the Cause for which He died.'

Thomas Hardy

* * *

1914

I. Peace

Now, God be thanked Who has matched us with His hour,
    And caught our youth, and wakened us from sleeping,
With hand made sure, clear eye, and sharpened power,
    To turn, as swimmers into cleanness leaping,
Glad from a world grown old and cold and weary,
    Leave the sick hearts that honour could not move,
And half-men, and their dirty songs and dreary,
    And all the little emptiness of love!

Oh! we, who have known shame, we have found release there,
   Where there's no ill, no grief, but sleep has mending,
   Naught broken save this body, lost but breath;
   Nothing to shake the laughing heart's long peace there
      But only agony, and that has ending;
      And the worst friend and enemy is but Death.

II. Safety

Dear! of all happy in the hour, most blest
   He who has found our hid security,
Assured in the dark tides of the world at rest,
   And heard our word, 'Who is so safe as we?'
We have found safety with all things undying,
   The winds, and morning, tears of men and mirth,
The deep night, and birds singing, and clouds flying,
   And sleep, and freedom, and the autumnal earth.
We have built a house that is not for Time's throwing.
   We have gained a peace unshaken by pain forever.
War knows no power. Safe shall be my going,
   Secretly armed against all death's endeavour;
Safe though all safety's lost; safe where men fall;
And if these poor limbs die, safest of all.

III. The Dead

Blow out, you bugles, over the rich Dead!
    There's none of these so lonely and poor of old,
    But, dying, has made us rarer gifts than gold.
These laid the world away; poured out the red
Sweet wine of youth; gave up the years to be
    Of work and joy, and that unhoped serene,
    That men call age; and those who would have been,
Their sons, they gave, their immortality.

Blow, bugles, blow! They brought us, for our dearth,
    Holiness, lacked so long, and Love, and Pain.
Honour has come back, as a king, to earth,
    And paid his subjects with a royal wage;
And nobleness walks in our ways again;
    And we have come into our heritage.

IV. The Dead

These hearts were woven of human joys and cares,
    Washed marvellously with sorrow, swift to mirth.

The years had given them kindness. Dawn was theirs,
    And sunset, and the colours of the earth.
These had seen movement, and heard music; known
    Slumber and waking; loved; gone proudly friended;
Felt the quick stir of wonder; sat alone;
    Touched flowers and furs and cheeks. All this is ended.

There are waters blown by changing winds to laughter
And lit by the rich skies, all day. And after,
    Frost, with a gesture, stays the waves that dance
And wandering loveliness. He leaves a white
    Unbroken glory, a gathered radiance,
A width, a shining peace, under the night.

V. The Soldier

If I should die, think only this of me:
    That there's some corner of a foreign field
That is forever England. There shall be
    In that rich earth a richer dust concealed;
A dust whom England bore, shaped, made aware,
    Gave, once, her flowers to love, her ways to roam,

A body of England's, breathing English air,
Washed by the rivers, blest by suns of home.
And think, this heart, all evil shed away,
A pulse in the eternal mind, no less
Gives somewhere back the thoughts by England given;
Her sights and sounds; dreams happy as her day;
And laughter, learnt of friends; and gentleness,
In hearts at peace, under an English heaven.

Rupert Brooke

* * *

RESURGAM

Exiled afar from youth and happy love,
If Death should ravish my fond spirit hence
I have no doubt but, like a homing dove,
It would return to its dear residence,
And through a thousand stars find out the road
Back into earthly flesh that was its loved abode.

Alan Seeger

THIS IS NO CASE OF PETTY RIGHT OR WRONG

This is no case of petty right or wrong
That politicians or philosophers
Can judge. I hate not Germans, nor grow hot
With love of Englishmen, to please newspapers.
Beside my hate for one fat patriot
My hatred of the Kaiser is love true:
A kind of god he is, banging a gong.
But I have not to choose between the two,
Or between justice and injustice. Dinned
With war and argument I read no more
Than in the storm smoking along the wind
Athwart the wood. Two witches' cauldrons roar.
From one the weather shall rise clear and gay;
Out of the other an England beautiful
And like her mother that died yesterday.
Little I know or care if, being dull,
I shall miss something that historians
Can rake out of the ashes when perchance
The phoenix broods serene above their ken.
But with the best and meanest Englishmen

I am one in crying, God save England, lest
We lose what never slaves and cattle blessed.
The ages made her that made us from dust:
She is all we know and live by, and we trust
She is good and must endure, loving her so:
And as we love ourselves we hate her foe.

Edward Thomas

* * *

RAINDROPS

Raindrops falling,
Falling on the reddened grass
Where through the night battle held full sway
Like Tears of God that drop in pity, then pass
To wash our guilt away.

H. Smalley Sarson

THE PARABLE OF THE OLD MAN AND THE YOUNG

So Abram rose, and clave the wood, and went,
And took the fire with him, and a knife.
And as they sojourned both of them together,
Isaac the first-born spake and said, 'My Father,
Behold the preparations, fire and iron,
But where the lamb, for this burnt-offering?'
Then Abram bound the youth with belts and straps,
And builded parapets and trenches there
And strechèd forth the knife to slay his son.
When lo! and Angel called him out of heaven,
Saying, 'Lay not thy hand upon the lad,
Neither do anything to him, thy son.
Behold! Caught in a thicket by its horns,
A Ram. Offer the Ram of Pride instead.'

But the old man would not so, but slew his son,
And half the seed of Europe, one by one.

Wilfred Owen

TO MY DAUGHTER BETTY, THE GIFT OF GOD

In wiser days, my darling rosebud, blown
To beauty proud as was your mother's prime,
In that desired, delayed, incredible time,
You'll ask why I abandoned you, my own,
And the dear heart that was your baby throne,
To dice with death. And oh! they'll give you rhyme
And reason: some will call the thing sublime,
And some decry it in a knowing tone.
So here, while the mad guns curse overhead,
And tired men sigh with mud for couch and floor,
Know that we fools, now with the foolish dead,
Died not for flag, nor King, nor Emperor,î
But for a dream, born in a herdsman's shed,
And for the secret Scripture of the poor.

T. H. Kettle

GONE, GONE AGAIN

Gone, gone again,
May, June, July,
And August gone,
Again gone by,

Not memorable
Save that I saw them go,
As past the empty quays
The rivers flow.

And now again,
In the harvest rain,
The Blenheim oranges
Fall grubby from the trees

As when I was young –
And when the lost one was here –
And when the war began
To turn young men to dung.

Look at the old house,
Outmoded, dignified,
Dark and untenanted,
With grass growing instead

Of the footsteps of life,
The friendliness, the strife;
In its beds have lain
Youth, love, age, and pain:

I am something like that;
Only I am not dead,
Still breathing and interested
In the house that is not dark –

I am something like that:
Not one pane to reflect the sun,
For the schoolboys to throw at –
They have broken every one.

Edward Thomas

VICTORY AND DEFEAT

Another year! – another deadly blow!

Another mighty Empire overthrown!

And We are left, or shall be left, alone;

The last that dare to struggle with the Foe.

The Destruction of the Sennacherib

The Assyrian came down like the wolf on the fold,
And his cohorts were gleaming in purple and gold;
And the sheen of their spears was like stars on the sea,
When the blue wave rolls nightly on deep Galilee.

Like the leaves of the forest when Summer is green,
That host with their banners at sunset were seen:
Like the leaves of the forest when Autumn hath blown,
That host on the morrow lay withered and strown.

For the Angel of Death spread his wings on the blast,
And breathed in the face of the foe as he passed;
And the eyes of the sleepers waxed deadly and chill,
And their hearts but once heaved, and forever grew still!

And there lay the steed with his nostril all wide,
But through it there rolled not the breath of his pride;
And the foam of his gasping lay white on the turf,
And cold as the spray of the rock-beating surf.

And there lay the rider distorted and pale,
With the dew on his brow, and the rust on his mail:

And the tents were all silent, the banners alone,
The lances unlifted, the trumpet unblown.

And the widows of Ashur are loud in their wail,
And the idols are broke in the temple of Baal;
And the might of the Gentile, unsmote by the sword,
Hath melted like snow in the glance of the Lord!

George Gordon, Lord Byron

* * *

LA BELLE DAME SANS MERCI

I

O what can ail thee, knight-at-arms,
    Alone and palely loitering?
The sedge has wither'd from the lake,
    And no birds sing.

II

O what can ail thee, knight-at-arms!
    So haggard and so woe-begone?
The squirrel's granary is full,
    And the harvest's done.

III

I see a lily on thy brow
      With anguish moist and fever dew,
And on thy cheeks a fading rose
      Fast withereth too.

IV

I met a lady in the meads,
      Full beautiful – a faery's child,
Her hair was long, her foot was light,
      And her eyes were wild.

V

I made a garland for her head,
      And bracelets too, and fragrant zone;
She look'd at me as she did love,
      And made sweet moan.

VI

I set her on my pacing steed,
      And nothing else saw all day long,
For sidelong would she bend, and sing
      A faery's song.

VII

She found me roots of relish sweet,
    And honey wild, and manna dew,
And sure in language strange she said –
    'I love thee true.'

VIII

She took me to her elfin grot,
    And there she wept, and sigh'd fill sore,
And there I shut her wild wild eyes
    With kisses four.

IX

And there she lulled me asleep,
    And there I dream'd – Ah! woe betide!
The latest dream I ever dream'd
    On the cold hill's side.

X

I saw pale kings and princes too,
    Pale warriors, death-pale were they all;
They cried – 'La Belle Dame sans Merci
    Hath thee in thrall!'

XI

I saw their starved lips in the gloam,
  With horrid warning gaped wide,
And I awoke and found me here,
  On the cold hill's side.

XII

And this is why I sojourn here,
  Alone and palely loitering,
Though the sedge is wither'd from the lake,
  And no birds sing.

John Keats

* * *

AN HORATIAN ODE UPON CROMWELL'S RETURN FROM IRELAND

The forward youth that would appear
Must now forsake his Muses dear,
  Nor in the shadows sing
  His numbers languishing.
'Tis time to leave the books in dust,
And oil th' unused armour's rust,

Removing from the wall
The corslet of the hall.
So restless Cromwell could not cease
In the inglorious arts of peace,
But through advent'rous war
Urged his active star.
And like the three-fork'd lightning, first
Breaking the clouds where it was nurst,
Did through his own side
His fiery way divide.
For 'tis all one to courage high,
The emulous or enemy;
And with such to enclose
Is more than to oppose.
Then burning through the air he went,
And palaces and temples rent;
And Cæsar's head at last
Did through his laurels blast.
'Tis madness to resist or blame
The force of angry Heaven's flame;
And, if we would speak true,
Much to the man is due,
Who from his private gardens where
He liv'd reserved and austere,

As if his highest plot
To plant the bergamot,
Could by industrious valour climb
To ruin the great work of time,
And cast the kingdom old
Into another mould.
Though justice against fate complain,
And plead the ancient rights in vain;
But those do hold or break
As men are strong or weak.
Nature that hateth emptiness
Allows of penetration less,
And therefore must make room
Where greater spirits come.
What field of all the civil wars
Where his were not the deepest scars?
And Hampton shows what part
He had of wiser art,
Where, twining subtle fears with hope,
He wove a net of such a scope
That Charles himself might chase
To Carisbrooke's narrow case,
That thence the royal actor borne
The tragic scaffold might adorn,

While round the armed bands
Did clap their bloody hands.
He nothing common did or mean
Upon that memorable scene,
But with his keener eye
The axe's edge did try;
Nor call'd the gods with vulgar spite
To vindicate his helpless right,
But bowed his comely head
Down as upon a bed.
This was that memorable hour
Which first assur'd the forced pow'r.
So when they did design
The Capitol's first line,
A bleeding head, where they begun,
Did fright the architects to run;
And yet in that the state
Foresaw its happy fate.
And now the Irish are asham'd
To see themselves in one year tam'd;
So much one man can do
That does both act and know.
They can affirm his praises best,
And have, though overcome, confest

How good he is, how just,
And fit for highest trust;
Nor yet grown stiffer with command,
But still in the republic's hand;
How fit he is to sway
That can so well obey.
He to the Commons' feet presents
A kingdom for his first year's rents;
And, what he may, forbears
His fame, to make it theirs,
And has his sword and spoils ungirt,
To lay them at the public's skirt.
So when the falcon high
Falls heavy from the sky,
She, having kill'd, no more does search
But on the next green bough to perch,
Where, when he first does lure,
The falc'ner has her sure.
What may not then our isle presume
While victory his crest does plume!
What may not others fear
If thus he crown each year!
A Cæsar he ere long to Gaul,

To Italy an Hannibal,
>> And to all states not free,
>> Shall climacteric be.
The Pict no shelter now shall find
Within his parti-colour'd mind;
>> But from this valour sad
>> Shrink underneath the plaid,
Happy if in the tufted brake
The English hunter him mistake,
>> Nor lay his hounds in near
>> The Caledonian deer.
But thou, the war's and fortune's son,
March indefatigably on;
>> And for the last effect
>> Still keep thy sword erect;
Besides the force it has to fright
The spirits of the shady night,
>> The same arts that did gain
>> A pow'r, must it maintain.

Andrew Marvell

ON THE LATE MASSACRE IN PIEDMONT

Avenge, O Lord, thy slaughter'd saints, whose bones
    Lie scattered on the Alpine mountains cold,
    Ev'n them who kept thy truth so pure of old,
    When all our fathers worshipp'd stocks and stones;
Forget not: in thy book record their groans
    Who were thy sheep, and in their ancient fold
    Slain by the bloody Piedmontese, that roll'd
    Mother with infant down the rocks. Their moans
The vales redoubl'd to the hills, and they
    To heaven. Their martyred blood and ashes sow
    O'er all th' Italian fields, where still doth sway
The triple Tyrant; that from these may grow
    A hundred-fold, who, having learnt thy way
Early may fly the Babylonian woe.

John Milton

* * *

THE BATTLE OF BLENHEIM

    It was a summer evening,
        Old Kaspar's work was done,
    And he before his cottage door

Was sitting in the sun,
And by him sported on the green
His little grandchild Wilhelmine.

She saw her brother Peterkin
Roll something large and round
Which he beside the rivulet
In playing there had found;
He came to ask what he had found,
That was so large, and smooth, and round.

Old Kaspar took it from the boy,
Who stood expectant by;
And then the old man shook his head,
And with a natural sigh,
"Tis some poor fellow's skull,' said he,
'Who fell in the great victory.

'I find them in the garden,
For there's many here about;
And often when I go to plough,
The ploughshare turns them out!
For many thousand men,' said he,
'Were slain in that great victory.'

'Now tell us what 'twas all about,'
　　Young Peterkin, he cries;
And little Wilhelmine looks up
　　With wonder-waiting eyes;
'Now tell us all about the war,
　　And what they fought each other for.'

'It was the English,' Kaspar cried,
　　'Who put the French to rout;
But what they fought each other for
　　I could not well make out;
But everybody said,' quoth he,
　　'That 'twas a famous victory.

'My father lived at Blenheim then,
　　Yon little stream hard by;
They burnt his dwelling to the ground,
　　And he was forced to fly;
So with his wife and child he fled,
　　Nor had he where to rest his head.

'With fire and sword the country round
　　Was wasted far and wide,
And many a childing mother then,
　　And newborn baby died;

But things like that, you know, must be
    At every famous victory.

'They said it was a shocking sight
    After the field was won;
For many thousand bodies here
    Lay rotting in the sun;
But things like that, you know, must be
    After a famous victory.

'Great praise the Duke of Marlbro won,
    And our good Prince Eugene.'
'Why, 'twas a very wicked thing!'
    Said little Wilhelmine.
'Nay, nay, my little girl,' quoth he,
    'It was a famous victory.

'And everybody praised the Duke
    Who this great fight did win.'
'But what good came of it at last?'
    Quoth little Peterkin.
'Why, that I cannot tell,' said he,
    'But 'twas a famous victory.'

Robert Southey

November, 1806

Another year! – another deadly blow!
Another mighty Empire overthrown!
And We are left, or shall be left, alone;
The last that dare to struggle with the Foe.
'Tis well! from this day forward we shall know
That in ourselves our safety must be sought;
That by our own right hands it must be wrought;
That we must stand unpropped, or be laid low.
O dastard whom such foretaste doth not cheer!
We shall exult, if they who rule the land
Be men who hold its many blessings dear,
Wise, upright, valiant; not a servile band,
Who are to judge of danger which they fear,
And honour which they do not understand.

William Wordsworth

Shiloh: A Requiem

(April, 1862)

Skimming lightly, wheeling still,
    The swallows fly low
Over the field in clouded days,
    The forest-field of Shiloh –
Over the field where April rain
Solaced the parched ones stretched in pain
Through the pause of night
That followed the Sunday fight
    Around the church of Shiloh –
The church so lone, the log-built one,
That echoed to many a parting groan
    And natural prayer
Of dying foemen mingled there –
Foeman at morn, but friends at eve –
    Fame or country least their care:
(What like a bullet can undeceive!)
    But now they lie low,
While over them the swallows skim,
    And all is hushed at Shiloh.

Herman Melville

My Portion is Defeat—today—

My Portion is Defeat—today—
A paler luck than Victory—
Less Paeans—fewer Bells—
The Drums don't follow Me—with tunes—
Defeat—a somewhat slower—means—
More Arduous than Balls—

'Tis populous with Bone and stain—
And Men too straight to stoop again—,
And Piles of solid Moan—
And Chips of Blank—in Boyish Eyes—
And scraps of Prayer—
And Death's surprise,
Stamped visible—in Stone—

There's somewhat prouder, over there—
The Trumpets tell it to the Air—
How different Victory
To Him who has it—and the One
Who to have had it, would have been
Contender—to die—

Emily Dickinson

The Conquered Banner

Furl that Banner, for 'tis weary;
Round its staff 'tis drooping dreary;
    Furl it, fold it – it is best;
For there's not a man to wave it,
And there's not a sword to save it,
And there's not one left to lave it
In the blood which heroes gave it;
And its foes now scorn and brave it;
    Furl it, hide it, – let it rest!

Take that banner down! 'tis tattered;
Broken is its shaft and shattered;
And the valiant hosts are scattered,
    Over whom it floated high.
Oh! 'tis hard for us to fold it,
Hard to think there's none to hold it,
Hard that those who once unrolled it
    Now must furl it with a sigh!

Furl that Banner – furl it sadly!
    Once ten thousands hailed it gladly,
And ten thousands wildly, madly,

Swore it should forever wave;
Swore that foeman's sword should never
Hearts like theirs entwined dissever,
Till that flag should float forever
  O'er their freedom or their grave!

Furl it; for the hands that grasped it,
And the hearts that fondly clasped it,
  Cold and dead are lying low;
And that Banner – it is trailing,
While around it sounds the wailing
  Of its people in their woe.

For, though conquered, they adore it –
  Love the cold, dead hands that bore it,
Weep for those who fell before it,
Pardon those who trailed and tore it;
But, oh! wildly they deplored it,
  Now who furl and fold it so!

Furl that Banner! True, 'tis gory,
Yet 'tis wreathed around with glory,
And 'twill live in song and story,

Though its folds are in the dust!
For its fame on brightest pages,
Penned by poets and by sages,
Shall go sounding down the ages –
      Furl its folds though now we must.

Furl that banner, softly, slowly!
Treat it gently – it is holy,
      For it droops above the dead.
Touch it not – unfold it never;
Let it droop there, furled forever, –
      For its people's hopes are fled!

Abram Joseph Ryan

* * *

THE LAND WHERE WE WERE DREAMING

Fair were our nation's visions! Oh, they were as grand
As ever floated out of Faerie land;
      Children were we in simple faith,
      But God-like children, whom, nor death,
Nor threat of danger drove from Honor's path,
      In the land where we were dreaming.

Proud were our men, as pride of birth could render,
As violets, our women pure and tender;
      And when they spoke, their voice did thrill
      Until at eve, whip-poor-will;
At morn the mocking bird was mute and still,
      In the land where we were dreaming.

And we had graves that covered more of glory,
Than ever taxed the lips of ancient story;
      And in our dream we wove the thread
      Of principles for which had bled,
And suffered long our own immortal dead,
      In the land where we were dreaming.

Though in our land we had both bond and free,
Both were content; and so God let them be; –
      'Till envy coveted our land,
      And those fair fields our valor won;
But little recked we, for we still slept on,
      In the land where we were dreaming.

Our sleep grew troubled and our dreams grew wild –
Red meteors flashed across our heaven's field;

Crimson the Moon; between the Twins
Barbed arrows fly, and then begins
Such strife as when disorder's Chaos reigns
O'er the land where we were dreaming.

Down from her sunlit height smiled Liberty,
And waved her hand in sign of Victory –
The world approved, and everywhere,
Except where growled the Russian bear,
The brave, the good, the just gave us their prayer,
For the land where we were dreaming.

We fancied that a Government was ours –
We challenged place among world's great powers;
We talked in sleep of Rank, Commission,
Until so lifelike grew our vision,
That he who dared to doubt but met derision
In the land where we were dreaming.

We looked on high: a banner there was seen,
Whose field was blanched, and spotless in its sheen –
Chivalry's cross its Union bears,
And vet'rans swearing by their scars

Vowed they would bear it through a hundred wars
    In the land where we were dreaming.

A hero came among us as we slept;
At first he knelt – then slowly rose and wept;
    Then gathering up a thousand spears
    He swept across the field of Mars;
Then bowed farewell and walked behind the stars –
    From the land where we were dreaming.

We looked again; another figure still
Gave hope, and nerved each individual will –
    Full of grandeur, clothed with power,
    Self-poised, erect, he ruled the hour
With stern, majestic sway – of strength a tower,
    In the land where we were dreaming.

As, while great Jove, in bronze, a warder God,
Gazed eastward from the Forum where he stood,
    Rome felt herself secure and free,
    So 'Richmond's safe,' we said, while we
Beheld a bronzed Hero – God-like Lee,
    In the land where we were dreaming.

As wakes the soldier when the alarum calls –
As wakes the mother when her infant falls –
  As starts the traveller when around
  His sleepy couch the fire-bells sound –
So woke our nation with a single bound
  In the land where we were dreaming.

Woe! woe is me! the startled mothers cried –
While we have slept our noble sons have died!
  Woe! woe is me! how strange and sad,
  That all our glorious vision's fled,
And left us nothing real but the dead,
  In the land where we were dreaming.

And are they really dead, our martyred slain?
No, dreamers! morn shall bid them rise again
  From every vale – from every height
  On which they *seemed* to die for right –
Their gallant spirits shall renew the fight
  In the land where we were dreaming.

   Daniel Bedinger Lucas

The Turning of the Tide

(February 27, 1900)

Storm, strong with all the bitter heart of hate,
Smote England, now nineteen dark years ago,
As when the tide's full wrath in seaward flow
Smites and bears back the swimmer. Fraud and fate
Were leagued against her: fear was fain to prate
Of honour in dishonour, pride brought low,
And humbleness whence holiness must grow,
And greatness born of shame to be so great.
The winter day that withered hope and pride
Shines now triumphal on the turning tide
That sets once more our trust in freedom free
That leaves a ruthless and a truthless foe
And all base hopes that hailed his cause laid low,
And England's name a shining light on land and sea.

Charles Algernon Swinburne

WHO MADE THE LAW?

Who made the Law that men should die in meadows?
Who spake the word that blood should splash in lanes?
Who gave it forth that gardens should be bone-yards?
Who spread the hills with flesh, and blood, and brains?
    Who made the Law?

Who made the Law that Death should stalk the village?
Who spake the word to kill among the sheaves,
Who gave it forth that death should lurk in hedgerows,
Who flung the dead among the fallen leaves?
    Who made the Law?

Those who return shall find that peace endures,
Find old things old, and knew the things they knew,
Walk in the garden, slumber by the fireside,
Share the peace of dawn, and dream amid the dew –
    Those who return.

Those who return shall till the ancient pastures,
Clean-hearted men shall guide the plough-horse reins,
Some shall grow apples and flowers in the valleys,
Some shall go courting in summer down the lanes –
    THOSE WHO RETURN.

But who made the Law? the Trees shall whisper to him:
'See, see the blood – the splashes on our bark!'
Walking the meadows, he shall hear bones crackle,
And fleshless mouths shall gibber in silent lanes at dark.
Who made the law?

Who made the Law? At noon upon the hillside
His ears shall hear a moan, his cheeks shall feel a breath,
And all along the valleys, past gardens, croft, and homesteads,
He who made the Law,
HE who made the Law,
HE who made the Law shall walk along with Death.
WHO made the Law?

Leslie Coulsen

* * *

A LETTER FROM ARAGON

This is a quiet sector of a quiet front.

We buried Ruiz in a new pine coffin,
But the shroud was too small and his washed feet stuck out.
The stink of his corpse came through the clean pine boards

And some of the bearers wrapped handkerchiefs round their faces.
Death was not dignified.
We hacked a ragged grave in the unfriendly earth
And fired a ragged volley over the grave.

You could tell from our listlessness, no one much missed him.

This is a quiet sector of a quiet front.
There is no poison gas and no H. E.

But when they shelled the other end of the village
And the streets were choked with dust
Women came screaming out of the crumbling houses,
Clutched under one arm the naked rump of an infant.
I thought: how ugly fear is.

This is a quiet sector of a quiet front.
Our nerves are steady; we all sleep soundly.

In the clean hospital bed, my eyes were so heavy
Sleep easily blotted out one ugly picture,
A wounded militiaman moaning on a stretcher,
Now out of danger, but still crying for water,
Strong against death, but unprepared for such pain.

This on a quiet front.

But when I shook hands to leave, an Anarchist worker

Said: 'Tell the workers of England

This was a war not of our own making

We did not seek it.

But if ever the Fascists again rule Barcelona

It will be as a heap of ruins with us workers beneath it.'

John Cornford

PEACE

Spirit whose work is done! spirit of dreadful hours!

Ere, departing, fade from my eyes your forests of bayonets;

Spirit of gloomiest fears and doubts, (yet onward ever unfaltering
*   pressing;)*

Spirit of many a solemn day, and many a savage scene! Electric spirit!

A FAREWELL TO ARMS

(To Queen Elizabeth)

His golden locks Time hath to silver turn'd;
    O Time too swift, O swiftness never ceasing!
His youth 'gainst time and age hath ever spurn'd,
    But spurn'd in vain; youth waneth by increasing:
Beauty, strength, youth, are flowers but fading seen;
    Duty, faith, love, are roots, and ever green.

His helmet now shall make a hive for bees;
    And, lovers' sonnets turn'd to holy psalms,
A man-at-arms must now serve on his knees,
    And feed on prayers, which are Age his alms:
But though from court to cottage he depart,
His Saint is sure of his unspotted heart.

And when he saddest sits in homely cell,
    He'll teach his swains this carol for a song, –
'Blest be the hearts that wish my sovereign well,
    Curst be the souls that think her any wrong,
Goddess, allow this agèd man his right
To be your beadsman now that was your knight.

George Peele

War

The victories of mind,
Are won for all mankind;
But war wastes what it wins,
Ends worse than it begins,
And is a game of woes,
Which nations always lose:
Though tyrant tyrant kill,
The slayer liveth still.

Ebenezer Elliott

* * *

Advice to a Raven in Russia

Black fool, why winter here? These frozen skies,
Worn by your wings and deafen'd by your cries,
Should warn you hence, where milder suns invite,
And day alternates with his mother night.
You fear perhaps your food will fail you there,
Your human carnage, that delicious fare
That lured you hither, following still your friend

The great Napoleon to the world's bleak end.
You fear, because the southern climes pour'd forth
Their clustering nations to infest the north,
Barvarians, Austrians, those who Drink the Po
And those who skirt the Tuscan seas below,
With all Germania, Neustria, Belgia, Gaul,
Doom'd here to wade thro slaughter to their fall,
You fear he left behind no wars, to feed
His feather'd cannibals and nurse the breed.
Fear not, my screamer, call your greedy train,
Sweep over Europe, hurry back to Spain,

You'll find his legions there; the valiant crew
Please best their master when they toil for you.
Abundant there they spread the country o'er
And taint the breeze with every nation's gore,
Iberian, Lussian, British widely strown,
But still more wide and copious flows their own.
Go where you will; Calabria, Malta, Greece,
Egypt and Syria still his fame increase,
Domingo's fatten'd isle and India's plains
Glow deep with purple drawn from Gallic veins.

No Raven's wing can stretch the flight so far
As the torn bandrols of Napoleon's war.
Choose then your climate, fix your best abode,
He'll make you deserts and he'll bring you blood.
How could you fear a dearth? have not mankind,
Tho slain by millions, millions left behind?
Has not CONSCRIPTION still the power to wield
Her annual faulchion o'er the human field?
A faithful harvester! or if a man
Escape that gleaner, shall he scape the BAN?

The triple BAN, that like the hound of hell
Gripes with three joles, to hold his victim well.
Fear nothing then, hatch fast your ravenous brood,
Teach them to cry to Bonaparte for food;
They'll be like you, of all his suppliant train,
The only class that never cries in vain.
For see what mutual benefits you lend!
(The surest way to fix the mutual friend)
While on his slaughter'd troops your tribes are fed,
You cleanse his camp and carry off his dead.
Imperial Scavenger! but now you know

Your work is vain amid these hills of snow.

His tentless troops are marbled thro with frost

And change to crystal when the breath is lost.

Mere trunks of ice, tho limb'd like human frames

And lately warm'd with life's endearing flames,

They cannot taint the air, the world impest,

Nor can you tear one fiber from their breast.

No! from their visual sockets, as they lie,

With beak and claws you cannot pluck an eye.

The frozen orb, preserving still its form,

Defies your talons as it braves the storm,

But stands and stares to God, as if to know

In what curst hands he leaves his world below.

Fly then, or starve; tho all the dreadful road

From Minsk to Moskow with their bodies strow'd

May count some Myriads, yet they can't suffice

To feed you more beneath these dreary skies.

Go back, and winter in the wilds of Spain;

Feast there awhile, and in the next campaign

Rejoin your master; for you'll find him then,

With his new million of the race of men,

Clothed in his thunders, all his flags unfurl'd,

Raging and storming o'er the prostrate world.
War after war his hungry soul requires,
State after State shall sink beneath his fires,
Yet other Spains in victim smoke shall rise
And other Moskows suffocate the skies,
Each land lie reeking with its people's slain
And not a stream run bloodless to the main.
Till men resume their souls, and dare to shed
Earth's total vengeance on the monster's head,
Hurl from his blood-built throne this king of woes,
Dash him to dust, and let the world repose.

Joel Barlow

* * *

CONCORD HYMN

By the rude bridge that arched the flood,
Their flag to April's breeze unfurled,
Here once the embattled farmers stood,
And fired the shot heard round the world.

The foe long since in silence slept;
Alike the conqueror silent sleeps;
And Time the ruined bridge has swept
Down the dark stream which seaward creeps.

On this green bank, by this soft stream,
We set today a votive stone;
That memory may their deed redeem,
When, like our sires, our sons are gone.

Spirit, that made those heroes dare,
To die, and leave their children free,
Bid Time and Nature gently spare
The shaft we raise to them and thee.

Ralph Waldo Emerson

THE ARSENAL AT SPRINGFIELD

This is the Arsenal. From floor to ceiling,
    Like a huge organ, rise the burnished arms;
But front their silent pipes no anthem pealing
    Startles the villages with strange alarms.

Ah! what a sound will rise, how wild and dreary,
    When the death-angel touches those swift keys!
What loud lament and dismal Miserere
    Will mingle with their awful symphonies

I hear even now the infinite fierce chorus,
    The cries of agony, the endless groan,
Which, through the ages that have gone before us,
    In long reverberations reach our own.

On helm and harness rings the Saxon hammer,
    Through Cimbric forest roars the Norseman's song,
And loud, amid the universal clamor,
    O'er distant deserts sounds the Tartar gong.

I hear the Florentine, who from his palace
     Wheels out his battle-bell with dreadful din,
And Aztec priests upon their teocallis
     Beat the wild war-drums made of serpent's skin;

The tumult of each sacked and burning village;
     The shout that every prayer for mercy drowns;
The soldiers' revels in the midst of pillage;
     The wail of famine in beleaguered towns;

The bursting shell, the gateway wrenched asunder,
     The rattling musketry, the clashing blade;
And ever and anon, in tones of thunder,
     The diapason of the cannonade.

Is it, O man, with such discordant noises,
     With such accursed instruments as these,
Thou drownest Nature's sweet and kindly voices,
     And jarrest the celestial harmonies?

Were half the power, that fills the world with terror,
     Were half the wealth, bestowed on camps and courts,
Given to redeem the human mind from error,
     There were no need of arsenals or forts:

The warrior's name would be a name abhorred!
    And every nation, that should lift again
Its hand against a brother, on its forehead
    Would wear forevermore the curse of Cain!

Down the dark future, through long generations,
    The echoing sounds grow fainter and then cease;
And like a bell, with solemn, sweet vibrations,
    I hear once more the voice of Christ say, 'Peace!'

Peace! and no longer from its brazen portals
    The blast of War's great organ shakes the skies!
But beautiful as songs of the immortals,
    The holy melodies of love arise.

Henry Wadsworth Longfellow

* * *

SPIRIT WHOSE WORK IS DONE

Spirit whose work is done! spirit of dreadful hours!
Ere, departing, fade from my eyes your forests of bayonets;
Spirit of gloomiest fears and doubts, (yet onward ever
    unfaltering pressing;)

Spirit of many a solemn day, and many a savage scene! Electric
spirit!

That with muttering voice, through the war now closed, like a
tireless phantom flitted,

Rousing the land with breath of flame, while you beat and beat
the drum;

– Now, as the sound of the drum, hollow and harsh to the last,
reverberates round me;

As your ranks, your immortal ranks, return, return from the
battles;

While the muskets of the young men yet lean over their
shoulders;

While I look on the bayonets bristling over their shoulders;

While those slanted bayonets, whole forests of them,
appearing in the distance, approach and pass on, returning
homeward,

Moving with steady motion, swaying to and fro, to the right and
left,

Evenly, lightly rising and falling, as the steps keep time;

– Spirit of hours I knew, all hectic red one day, but pale as death
next day;

Touch my mouth, ere you depart – press my lips close!

Leave me your pulses of rage! bequeath them to me! fill me with
 currents convulsive!
Let them scorch and blister out of my chants, when you are
 gone;
Let them identify you to the future, in these songs.

Walt Whitman

* * *

THE BLUE AND THE GRAY

By the flow of the inland river,
 Whence the fleets of iron have fled,
Where the blades of the grave-grass quiver,
 Asleep are the ranks of the dead:
Under the sod and the dew,
 Waiting the judgment-day;
Under the one, the Blue,
 Under the other, the Gray.

These in the robings of glory,
 Those in the gloom of defeat,
All with the battle-blood gory,
 In the dusk of eternity meet:

Under the sod and the dew,
    Waiting the judgment-day;
Under the laurel, the Blue,
    Under the willow, the Gray.

From the silence of sorrowful hours
    The desolate mourners go,
Lovingly laden with flowers
    Alike for the friend and the foe:
    Under the sod and the dew,
        Waiting the judgment-day;
    Under the roses, the Blue,
        Under the lilies, the Gray.

So with an equal splendor,
    The morning sun-rays fall,
With a touch impartially tender,
    On the blossoms blooming for all:
    Under the sod and the dew,
        Waiting the judgment-day;
    Broidered with gold, the Blue,
        Mellowed with gold, the Gray.

So, when the summer calleth,
   On forest and field of grain,
With an equal murmur falleth
   The cooling drip of the rain:
      Under the sod and the dew,
         Waiting the judgment-day;
      Wet with the rain, the Blue,
         Wet with the rain, the Gray.

Sadly, but not with upbraiding,
   The generous deed was done,
In the storm of the years that are fading
   No braver battle was won:
      Under the sod and the dew,
         Waiting the judgment-day;
      Under the blossoms, the Blue,
         Under the garlands, the Gray.

No more shall the war cry sever,
   Or the winding rivers be red;
They banish our anger forever
   When they laurel the graves of our dead!
      Under the sod and the dew,

Waiting the judgment-day;
Love and tears for the Blue,
Tears and love for the Gray.

Francis Miles Finch

* * *

ASHES OF GLORY

Fold up the gorgeous silken sun,
    By bleeding martyrs blest,
And heap the laurels it has won
    Above its place of rest.

No trumpet's note need harshly blast –
    No drum funereal roll –
Nor trailing sables drape the bier
    That frees a dauntless soul!

It lived with Lee, and decked his brow
    From fate's empyreal Palm;
It sleeps the sleep of Jackson now –
    As spotless and as calm.

It was outnumbered – not outdone;
    And they shall shuddering tell
Who struck the blow, its latest gun
    Flashed ruin as it fell.

Sleep, shrouded Ensign! Not the breeze
    That smote the victor tar
With death across the heaving seas
    Of fiery Trafalgar;

Not Arthur's knights, amid the gloom
    Their knightly deeds have starred;
Nor Gallic Henry's matchless plume,
    Nor peerless-born Bayard;

Not all that antique fables fame,
    And orient dreams disgorge;
Nor yet the silver cross of Spain,
    And lion of St. George,

Can bid thee pale! Proud emblem, still
    Thy crimson glory shines
Beyond the lengthened shades that fill
    Their proudest kingly lines.

Sleep in thine own historic night!
And be thy blazoned scroll,
A Warrior's Banner takes its flight,
To greet the warrior's soul!

Augustus Julian Requier

* * *

RECONCILIATION

Word over all, beautiful as the sky!

Beautiful that war, and all its deeds of carnage, must in time be
utterly lost;

That the hands of the sisters Death and Night, incessantly softly
wash again, and ever again, this soil'd world:

…For my enemy is dead – a man divine as myself is dead;

I look where he lies, white-faced and still, in the coffin – I draw
near;

I bend down, and touch lightly with my lips the white face in
the coffin.

Walt Whitman

A Year's 'Casualties'

Slain as they lay by the secret, slow,
Pitiless hand of an unseen foe,
Two score thousand old soldiers have crossed
The river to join the loved and lost.
In the space of a year their spirits fled,
Silent and white, to the camp of the dead.

One after one, they fall asleep
And the pension agents awake to weep,
And orphaned statesmen are loud in their wail
As the souls flit by on the evening gale.
O Father of Battles, pray give us release
From the horrors of peace, the horrors of peace!

Ambrose Bierce

* * *

Soldier from the Wars Returning

Soldier from the wars returning,
Spoiler of the taken town,

Here is ease that asks not earning;
    Turn you in and sit you down.

Peace is come and wars are over,
    Welcome you and welcome all,
While the charger crops the clover
    And his bridle hangs in stall.

Now no more of winters biting,
    Filth in trench from fall to spring,
Summers full of sweat and fighting
    For the Kesar or the King.

Rest you, charger, rust you, bridle;
    Kings and kesars, keep your pay;
Soldier, sit you down and idle
    At the inn of night for aye.

A. E. Housman

ASTRONOMY

The Wain upon the northern steep
Descends and lifts away.
Oh I will sit me down and weep
For bones in Africa.
For pay and medals, name and rank,
Things that he has not found,
He hove the Cross to heaven and sank
The pole-star underground.

And now he does not even see
Signs of the nadir roll
At night over the ground where he
Is buried with the pole.

A. E. Housman

* * *

THE MAN WITH THE WOODEN LEG

There was a man lived quite near us;
He had a wooden leg and a goldfinch in a green cage.
His name was Farkey Anderson,

And he'd been in a war to get his leg.
We were very sad about him,
Because he had such a beautiful smile
And was such a big man to live in a very small house.
When he walked on the road his leg did not matter so
much;
But when he walked in his little house
It made an ugly noise.
Little Brother said his goldfinch sang the loudest of all
birds,
So that he should not hear his poor leg
And feel too sorry about it.

Katherine Mansfield

* * *

THE NEXT WAR

War's a joke for me and you,
While we know such dreams are true.
SIEGFRIED SASSOON

Out there, we've walked quite friendly up to Death;
    Sat down and eaten with him, cool and bland –

Pardoned his spilling mess-tins in our hand.
We've sniffed the green thick odour of his breath –
Our eyes wept, but our courage didn't writhe.

   He's spat at us with bullets and he's coughed
      Shrapnel. We chorused when he sang aloft;
We whistled while he shaved us with his scythe.

Oh, Death was never enemy of ours!
      We laughed at him, we leagued with him, old chum.
No soldier's paid to kick against His powers.
We laughed, knowing that better men would come,
And greater wars: when each proud fighter brags
He wars on Death – or lives; not men – for flags.

Wilfred Owen

* * *

ELEGY IN COUNTRY CHURCHYARD

The men that worked for England
They have their graves at home:
And bees and birds of England
About the cross can roam.

But they that fought for England,
Following a falling star,
Alas, alas for England
They have their graves afar.

And they that rule in England,
In stately conclave met,
Alas, alas for England,
They have no graves as yet.

G. K. Chesterton

* * *

Epitaphs to the War

1914–1918

'EQUALITY OF SACRIFICE'
A 'I was a Have.' B. 'I was a "have-not".'
(*Together*.) 'What hast thou given which I gave not?'

A SERVANT
We were together since the War began.
He was my servant – and the better man.

A SON

My son was killed while laughing at some jest. I would I knew
What it was, and it might serve me in a time when jests are few.

AN ONLY SON

I have slain none except my Mother. She
(Blessing her slayer) died of grief for me.

EX-CLERK

Pity not! The army gave
Freedom to a timid slave:
In which freedom did he find
Strength of body, will, and mind:
By which strength he came to prove
Mirth, companionship, and love:
For which love to death he went:
In which death he lies content.

THE WONDER

Body and spirit I surrendered whole
To harsh instructors – and received a soul...
If mortal man could change me through and through
From all I was – what may the God not do?

HINDU SEPOY OF FRANCE

This man in his own country prayed we know not to what
   powers.
We pray them to reward him for his bravery in ours.

THE COWARD

I could not look on death, which being known,
Men led me to him, blindfold and alone.

SHOCK

My name, my speech, my self I had forgot.
My wife and children came – I knew them not.
I died. My mother followed. At her call
And on her bosom I remembered all.

A GRAVE NEAR CAIRO

Gods of the Nile, should this stout fellow here
Get out – get out! He knows not shame nor fear.

PELICANS IN THE WILDERNESS
(A Grave near Halfa)

The blown sand heaps on me, that none may learn
Where I am laid for whom my children grieve...

O wings that beat at dawning, ye return
Out of the desert to your young at eve!

TWO CANADIAN MEMORIALS

I

We giving all gained all.
Neither lament us nor praise.
Only in all things recall,
It is Fear, not Death that slays.

II

From little towns in a far land we came,
To save our honour and a world aflame.
By little towns in a far land we sleep;
And trust that world we won for you to keep!

THE FAVOUR

Death favoured me from the first, well knowing I could not endure
To wait on him day by day. He quitted my betters and came
Whistling over the fields, and, when he had made all sure,
'Thy line is at end,' he said, 'but at least I have saved its name.'

THE BEGINNER
On the first hour of my first day
In the front trench I fell.
(Children in boxes at a play
Stand up to watch it well.)

R. A. F. (AGED EIGHTEEN)
Laughing through clouds, his milk-teeth still unshed,
Cities and men he smote from overhead.
His deaths delivered, he returned to play
Childlike, with childish things now put away.

THE REFINED MAN
I was of delicate mind. I stepped aside for my needs,
Disdaining the common office. I was seen from afar and
    killed...
How is this matter for mirth? Let each man be judged by his
    deeds.
I have laid my price to live with myself on the terms that I willed.

NATIVE WATER-CARRIER (M. E. F.)
Prometheus brought down fire to men.
    This brought up water.

The Gods are jealous – now, as then,
Giving no quarter.

BOMBED IN LONDON

On land and sea I strove with anxious care
To escape conscription. It was in the air!

THE SLEEPY SENTINEL

Faithless the watch that I kept: now I have none to keep.
I was slain because I slept: now I am slain I sleep.
Let no man reproach me again; whatever watch is unkept –
I sleep because I am slain. They slew me because I slept.

BATTERIES OUT OF AMMUNITION

If any mourn us in the workshop, say
We died because the shift kept holiday.

COMMON FORM

If any question why we died,
Tell them, because our fathers lied.

A DEAD STATESMAN

I could not dig: I dared not rob:
Therefore I lied to please the mob.
Now all my lies are proved untrue
And I must face the men I slew.
What tale shall serve me here among
Mine angry and defrauded young?

THE REBEL

If I had clamoured at Thy Gate
For gift of Life on Earth,
And, thrusting through the souls that wait,
Flung headlong into birth –
Even then, even then, for gin and snare
About my pathway spread,
Lord, I had mocked Thy thoughtful care
Before I joined the Dead!
But now?... I was beneath Thy hand
Ere yet the planets came.
And now – though planets pass, I stand
The witness to Thy shame!

THE OBEDIENT

Daily, though no ears attended,
Did my prayers arise.
Daily, though no fire descended
Did I sacrifice.
Though my darkness did not lift,
Though I faced no lighter odds,
Though the Gods bestowed no gift,
None the less,
None the less, I served the Gods!

A DRIFTER OFF TARENTUM

He from the wind-bitten north with ship and companions
descended.

Searching for eggs of death spawned by invisible hulls.

Many he found and drew forth. Of a sudden the fishery
ended

In flame and a clamorous breath not new to the eye-pecking
gulls.

DESTROYERS IN COLLUSION

For Fog and Fate no charm is found
To lighten or amend.
I, hurrying to my bride, was drowned –
Cut down by my best friend.

CONVOY ESCORT

I was a shepherd to fools
Causelessly bold or afraid.
They would not abide by my rules.
Yet they escaped. For I stayed.

UNKNOWN FEMALE CORPSE

Headless, lacking foot and hand,
Horrible I come to land.
I beseech all women's sons
Know I was a mother once.

RAPED AND REVENGED

One used and butchered me: another spied
Me broken – for which thing an hundred died.
So it was learned among the heathen hosts
How much a freeborn woman's favour costs.

SALONIKAN GRAVE

I have watched a thousand days
Push out and crawl into night
Slowly as tortoises.
Now I, too, follow these.
It is fever, and not the fight –
Time, not battle, – that slays.

THE BRIDEGROOM

Call me not false, beloved,
        If, from thy scarce-known breast
So little time removed,
        In other arms I rest.

For this more ancient bride
        Whom coldly I embrace
Was constant at my side
        Before I saw thy face.

Our marriage, often set –
        By miracle delayed –
At last is consummate,
        And cannot be unmade.

Live, then, whom life shall cure.
Almost, of memory,
And leave us to endure
Its immortality.

VAD (MEDITERRANEAN)

Ah, would swift ships had never been, for then we ne'er had
found,
These harsh Aegean rocks between, this little virgin drowned,
Whom neither spouse nor child shall mourn, but men she
nursed through pain
And – certain keels for whose return the heathen look in vain.

ACTORS

On a Memorial Tablet in Holy Trinity Church, Stratford-On-Avon
We counterfeited once for your disport
Men's joy and sorrow; but our day has passed.
We pray you pardon all where we fell short –
Seeing we were your servants to this last.

JOURNALISTS

On a Panel in the Hall of the Institute of Journalists
We have served our day.

Rudyard Kipling

REMEMBRANCE

O too lightly he threw down his cap

One day when the breeze threw petals from the trees.

The unflowering wall sprouted with guns,

Machine-gun anger quickly scythed the grasses;

Flags and leaves fell from hands and branches;

The tweed cap rotted in the nettles.

THE LAMENT OF MAEV LEITH-DHERG

For Cuchorb: Son of Moghcorb, King of Ireland

Raise the Cromlech high!
     MacMoghcorb is slain,
And other men's renown
     Has leave to live again.

Cold at last he lies
     Neath the burial-stone;
All the blood he shed
     Could not save his own.

Stately-strong he went,
     Through his nobles all
When we paced together
     Up the banquet-hall.

Dazzling white as lime
     Was his body fair,
Cherry-red his cheeks,
     Raven-black his hair.

Razor-sharp his spear,
     And the shield he bore,
High as champion's head –
     His arm was like an oar.

Never aught but truth
     Spake my noble king;
Valour all his trust
     In all his warfaring.

As the forkéd pole
     Holds the roof-tree's weight,
So my hero's arm
     Held the battle straight.

Terror went before him,
     Death behind his back;
Well the wolves of Erinn
     Knew his chariot's track.

Seven bloody battles
     He broke upon his foes;
In each a hundred heroes
     Fell beneath his blows.

Once he fought at Fossud,
      Thrice at Ath-finn-Fail;
'Twas my king that conquered
      At bloody Ath-an-Scail.

At the boundary Stream
      Fought the Royal Hound,
And for Bernas battle
      Stands his name renowned.

Here he fought with Leinster –
      Last of all his frays
On the Hill of Cucorb's Fate
      High his Cromlech raise.

Anonymous

* * *

AN EPITAPH ON CLERE

Norfolk sprung thee, *Lambeth* holds thee dead;
Clere, of the County of *Cleer-mont*, though hight
Within the Womb of *Ormond's* Race thou bred,
And sawest thy Cosin Crowned in thy Sight;
Shelton for love, *Surry* for Lord thou chase;
Aye, me! whilst Life did last that League was tend
Tracing whose Steps, thou sawest *Kelsall* blaze,

Laundersey burnt, and batter'd *Bullen* render;
At *Muttrel* Gates, hopeless of all Re-cure
Thine Earl, half Dead, gave in thy Hand his Will;
Which Cause did thee, this pining Death procure,
E're Summers, Seven times Seven thou, could'st fulfill.
    Ah! Clere, if Love had booted, Care, or Cost,
    Heaven had not won, nor Earth so timely lost.

Henry Howard

* * *

THE BURIAL OF SIR JOHN MOORE AFTER CORUNNA

Not a drum was heard, not a funeral note,
    As his corse to the rampart we hurried;
Not a soldier discharged his farewell shot
    O'er the grave where our hero we buried.

We buried him darkly at dead of night,
    The sods with our bayonets turning,
By the struggling moonbeam's misty light
    And the lanthorn dimly burning.

No useless coffin enclosed his breast,
    Not in sheet or in shroud we wound him;

But he lay like a warrior taking his rest
  With his martial cloak around him.

Few and short were the prayers we said,
  And we spoke not a word of sorrow;
But we steadfastly gazed on the face that was dead,
  And we bitterly thought of the morrow.

We thought, as we hollow'd his narrow bed
  And smooth'd down his lonely pillow,
That the foe and the stranger would tread o'er his head,
  And we far away on the billow!

Lightly they'll talk of the spirit that's gone,
  And o'er his cold ashes upbraid him –
But little he'll reck, if they let him sleep on
  In the grave where a Briton has laid him.

But half of our heavy task was done
  When the clock struck the hour for retiring;
And we heard the distant and random gun
  That the foe was sullenly firing.

Slowly and sadly we laid him down,
    From the field of his fame fresh and gory;
We carved not a line, and we raised not a stone,
    But we left him alone with his glory.

Charles Wolfe

* * *

BROCK

One voice, one people, one in heart
    And soul and feeling and desire.
    Re-light the smouldering martial fire
    And sound the mute trumpet! Strike the lyre!
    The hero dead cannot expire:
The dead still play their part.

Raise high the monumental stone!
    A nation's fealty is theirs,
    And we are the rejoicing heirs,
    The honoured sons of sires whose cares
    We take upon us unawares
As freely as our own.

We boast not of the victory,
But render homage, deep and just,
To his – to their – immortal dust,
Who proved so worthy of their trust;
No lofty pile nor sculptured bust
Can herald their degree.

No tongue can blazon forth their fame –
The cheers that stir the sacred hill
Are but mere promptings of the will
That conquered them, that conquers still;
And generations yet shall thrill
At Brock's remembered name.

Some souls are the Hesperides
Heaven sends to guard the golden age,
Illumining the historic page
With record of their pilgrimage.
True martyr, hero, poet, sage, –
And he was one of these.

Each in his lofty sphere, sublime,
Sits crowned above the common throng:
Wrestling with some pythonic wrong

In prayer, in thunders, thought or song,
Briareus-limbed, they sweep along,
The Typhons of the time.

Charles Sangster

* * *

ODE

Sleep sweetly in your humble graves,
Sleep, martyrs of a fallen cause;
Though yet no marble column craves
The pilgrim here to pause.

In seeds of laurel in the earth,
The blossom of your fame is blown,
And somewhere, waiting for its birth,
The shaft is in the stone.

Meanwhile, behalf the tardy years,
Which keep in trust your storied tombs,
Behold your sisters bring their tears,
And these memorial blooms.

Small tributes but your shades will smile
      More proudly on these wreaths today,
Than when some cannon-moulded pile
      Shall overlook this bay.

Stoop, angels, thither from the skies,
      There is no holier spot of ground
Than where defeated valor lies,
      By mourning beauty crowned.

Henry Timrod

* * *

THE UNKNOWN DEAD

The rain is plashing on my sill,
But all the winds of Heaven are still;
And so it falls with that dull sound
Which thrills us in the churchyard ground,
When the first spadeful drops like lead
Upon the coffin of the dead.
Beyond my streaming window-pane,
I cannot see the neighboring vane,
Yet from its old familiar tower

The bell comes, muffled, through the shower.
What strange and unsuspected link
Of feeling touched, has made me think –
While with a vacant soul and eye
I watch that gray and stony sky –
Of nameless graves on battle-plains
Washed by a single winter's rains,
Where, some beneath Virginian hills,
And some by green Atlantic rills,
Some by the waters of the West,
A myriad unknown heroes rest.
Ah! not the chiefs, who, dying, see
Their flags in front of victory,
Or, at their life-blood's noble cost
Pay for a battle nobly lost,
Claim from their monumental beds
The bitterest tears a nation sheds.

Beneath yon lonely mound – the spot
By all save some fond few forgot –
Lie the true martyrs of the fight
Which strikes for freedom and for right.
Of them, their patriot zeal and pride,
The lofty faith that with them died,

No grateful page shall farther tell
Than that so many bravely fell;
And we can only dimly guess
What worlds of all this world's distress,
What utter woe, despair, and dearth,
Their fate has brought to many a hearth.
Just such a sky as this should weep
Above them, always, where they sleep;
Yet, haply, at this very hour,
Their graves are like a lover's bower;
And Nature's self, with eyes unwet,
Oblivious of the crimson debt
To which she owes her April grace,
Laughs gayly o'er their burial-place.

Henry Timrod

O Captain! My Captain!

O Captain! my Captain! our fearful trip is done,
The ship has weather'd every rack, the prize we sought is won,
The port is near, the bells I hear, the people all exulting,
While follow eyes the steady keel, the vessel grim and daring;
  But O heart, heart, heart,
    O the bleeding drops of red,
      Where on the deck my Captain lies,
       Fallen cold and dead.

O Captain! my Captain! rise up and hear the bells;
Rise up – for you the flag is flung – for you the bugle trills,
For you bouquets and ribbon'd wreaths – for you the shores
 a-crowding,
For you they call, the swaying mass, their eager faces turning;
  Here Captain, dear father,
    This arm beneath your head,
      It is some dream that on the deck
       You've fallen cold and dead.

My captain does not answer, his lips are pale and still,
My father does not feel my arm, he has no pulse nor will,
The ship is anchor'd safe and sound, its voyage closed and done,

From fearful trip the victor ship comes in with object won;
Exult O shores, and ring O bells,
But I, with mournful tread,
Walk the deck my Captain lies,
Fallen cold and dead.

Walt Whitman

* * *

ROBERT E. LEE

A gallant foeman in the fight,
A brother when the fight was o'er,
The hand that led the host with might
The blessed torch of learning bore.

No shriek of shells nor roll of drums,
No challenge fierce, resounding far,
When reconciling Wisdom comes
To heal the cruel wounds of war.

Thought may the minds of men divide,
Love makes the heart of nations one,

And so, the soldier grave beside,
We honor thee, Virginia's son.

Julia Ward Howe

* * *

To E. S. SALOMON

Who in a Memorial Day oration protested bitterly against decorating the graves of Confederate dead.

What! Salomon! such words from you,
Who call yourself a soldier? Well,
The Southern brother where he fell
Slept all your base oration through.

Alike to him – he cannot know
Your praise or blame: as little harm
Your tongue can do him as your arm
A quarter-century ago.

The brave respect the brave. The brave
Respect the dead; but you – you draw

That ancient blade, the ass's jaw,
And shake it o'er a hero's grave.

Are you not he who makes today
    A merchandise of old reknown
    Which he persuades this easy town
He won in battle far away?

Nay, those the fallen who revile
    Have ne'er before the living stood
    And stoutly made their battle good
And greeted danger with a smile.

What if the dead whom still you hate
    Were wrong? Are you so surely right?
    We know the issues of the fight –
The sword is but an advocate.

Men live and die, and other men
    Arise with knowledges diverse:
    What seemed a blessing seems a curse,
And Now is still at odds with Then.

The years go on, the old comes back
      To mock the new – beneath the sun
      Is nothing new; ideas run
Recurrent in an endless track.

What most we censure, men as wise
      Have reverently practiced; nor
      Will future wisdom fail to war
On principles we dearly prize.

We do not know – we can but deem,
      And he is loyalest and best
      Who takes the light full on his breast
And follows it throughout the dream.

The broken light, the shadows wide –
      Behold the battle-field displayed!
      God save the vanquished from the blade,
The victor from the victor's pride.

If, Salomon, the blessed dew
      That falls upon the Blue and Gray
      Is powerless to wash away
The sin of differing from you.

Remember how the flood of years
    Has rolled across the erring slain;
    Remember, too, the cleansing rain
Of widows' and of orphans' tears.

The dead are dead – let that atone:
    And though with equal hand we strew
    The blooms on saint and sinner too,
Yet God will know to choose his own.

The wretch, whate'er his life and lot,
    Who does not love the harmless dead
    With all his heart and all his head –
May God forgive him, I shall not.

When, Salomon, you come to quaff
    The Darker Cup with meeker face,
    I, loving you at last, shall trace
Upon your tomb this epitaph:

'Draw near, ye generous and brave –
    Kneel round this monument and weep

For one who tried in vain to keep
A flower from a soldier's grave.'

Ambrose Bierce

* * *

To L. H. B. (1894–1915)

Last night for the first time since you were dead
I walked with you, my brother, in a dream.
We were at home again beside the stream
Fringed with tall berry bushes, white and red.
'Don't touch them: they are poisonous,' I said.
But your hand hovered, and I saw a beam
Of strange, bright laughter flying round your head
And as you stooped I saw the berries gleam.
'Don't you remember? We called them Dead Man's Bread!'
I woke and heard the wind moan and the roar
Of the dark water tumbling on the shore.
Where – where is the path of my dream for my eager feet?
By the remembered stream my brother stands
Waiting for me with berries in his hands…
'These are my body. Sister, take and eat.'

Katherine Mansfield

To His Love

He's gone, and all our plans
      Are useless indeed.
We'll walk no more on Cotswolds
      Where the sheep feed
      Quietly and take no heed.

His body that was so quick
      Is not as you
Knew it, on Severn River
      Under the blue
      Driving our small boat through.

You would not know him now…
      But still he died
Nobly, so cover him over
      With violets of pride
      Purple from Severn side.

Cover him, cover him soon!
      And with thick-set
Masses of memoried flowers –

Hide that red wet
Thing I must somehow forget.

Ivor Gurney

* * *

GOD! HOW I HATE YOU, YOU YOUNG CHEERFUL MEN

God! How I hate you, you young cheerful men,
Whose pious poetry blossoms on your graves
As soon as you are in them, nurtured up
By the salt of your corruption, and the tears
Of mothers, local vicars, college deans,
And flanked by prefaces and photographs
From all you minor poet friends – the fools –
Who paint their sentimental elegies
Where sure, no angel treads; and, living, share
The dead's brief immortality

                              Oh Christ!
To think that one could spread the ductile wax
Of his fluid youth to Oxford's glowing fires
And take her seal so ill! Hark how one chants –
'Oh happy to have lived these epic days' –
'These epic days'! And he'd been to France,

And seen the trenches, glimpsed the huddled dead
In the periscope, hung in the rusting wire:
Choked by their sickly fœtor, day and night
Blown down his throat: stumbled through ruined hearths,
Proved all that muddy brown monotony,
Where blood's the only coloured thing. Perhaps
Had seen a man killed, a sentry shot at night,
Hunched as he fell, his feet on the firing-step,
His neck against the back slope of the trench,
And the rest doubled up between, his head
Smashed like an egg-shell, and the warm grey brain
Spattered all bloody on the parados:
Had flashed a torch on his face, and known his friend,
Shot, breathing hardly, in ten minutes – gone!
Yet still God's in His heaven, all is right
In the best possible of worlds. The woe,
Even His scaled eyes must see, is partial, only
A seeming woe, we cannot understand.
God loves us, God looks down on this out strife
And smiles in pity, blows a pipe at times
And calls some warriors home. We do not die,
God would not let us, He is too 'intense',
Too 'passionate', a whole day sorrows He

Because a grass-blade dies. How rare life is!
On earth, the love and fellowship of men,
Men sternly banded: banded for what end?
Banded to maim and kill their fellow men –
For even Huns are men. In heaven above
A genial umpire, a good judge of sport,
Won't let us hurt each other! Let's rejoice
God keeps us faithful, pens us still in fold.
Ah, what a faith is ours (almost, it seems,
Large as a mustard-seed) – we trust and trust,
Nothing can shake us! Ah, how good God is
To suffer us to be born just now, when youth
That else would rust, can slake his blade in gore,
Where very God Himself does seem to walk
The bloody fields of Flanders He so loves!

Arthur Graeme West

* * *

ICI REPOSE

A little cross of weather-silvered wood,
Hung with a garish wreath of tinselled wire,
And on it carved a legend – thus it runs:

'*Ici Repose*—' Add what name you will
And multiply by thousands: in the fields,
Along the roads, beneath the trees – one here,
A dozen there, to each its simple tale
Of one more jewel threaded star-like on
The sacrificial rosary of France.
And as I read and read again those words,
Those simple words, they took a mystic sense;
And from the glamour of an alien tongue
They wove insistent music in my brain,
Which, in a twilight hour, when all the guns
Were silent, shaped itself to song.

O happy dead! Who sleep embalmed in glory,
        Safe from corruption, purified by fire, –
Ask you our pity? – ours, mud-grimed and gory,
        Who still must grimly strive, grimly desire?

You have outrun the reach of our endeavour,
        Have flown beyond our most exalted quest, –
Who prate of Faith and Freedom, knowing ever
        That all we really fight for's just – a rest,

The rest that only Victory can bring us —
    Or Death, which throws us brother-like by you —
The civil commonplace in which 'twill fling us
    To neutralize our then too martial hue.

But you have rest from every tribulation
    Even in the midst of war; you sleep serene,
Pinnacled on the sorrow of a nation,
    In cerements of sacrificial sheen.

Oblivion cannot claim you: our heroic
    War-lustred moment, as our youth, will pass
To swell the dusty hoard of Time the Stoic,
    That gathers cobwebs in the nether glass.

We shall grow old, and tainted with the rotten
    Effluvia of the peace we fought to win,
The bright deeds of our youth will be forgotten,
    Effaced by later failure, sloth, or sin;

But you have conquered Time, and sleep forever,
    Like gods, with a white halo on your brows —

Your souls our lode-stars, your death-crowned endeavour
That spur that holds the nations to their vows.

Bernard Freeman Trotter

* * *

DEAD MAN'S DUMP

The plunging limbers over the shattered track
Racketed with their rusty freight,
Stuck out like many crowns of thorns,
And the rusty stakes like sceptres old
To stay the flood of brutish men
Upon our brothers dear.

The wheels lurched over sprawled dead
But pained them not, though their bones crunched,
Their shut mouths made no moan,
They lie there huddled, friend and foeman,
Man born of man, and born of woman,
And shells go crying over them
From night till night and now.

Earth has waited for them
All the time of their growth
Fretting for their decay:
Now she has them at last!
In the strength of their strength
Suspended – stopped and held.

What fierce imaginings their dark souls lit?
Earth! have they gone into you?
Somewhere they must have gone,
And flung on your hard back
Is their souls' sack,
Emptied of God-ancestralled essences.
Who hurled them out? Who hurled?

None saw their spirits' shadow shake the grass,
Or stood aside for the half-used life to pass
Out of those doomed nostrils and the doomed mouth,
When the swift iron burning bee
Drained the wild honey of their youth.

What of us who, flung on the shrieking pyre,
Walk, our usual thoughts untouched,

Our lucky limbs as on ichor fed,
Immortal seeming ever?
Perhaps when the flames beat loud on us,
A fear may choke in our veins
And the startled blood may stop.

The air is loud with death,
The dark air spurts with fire
The explosions ceaseless are.
Timelessly now, some minutes past,
These dead strode time with vigorous life,
Till the shrapnel called 'an end!'
But not to all. In bleeding pangs
Some borne on stretchers dreamed of home,
Dear things, war blotted from their hearts.

A man's brains splattered on
A stretcher-bearer's face;
His shook shoulders slipped their load,
But when they bent to look again
The drowning soul was sunk too deep
For human tenderness.

They left this dead with the older dead,
Stretched at the crossroads.
Burnt black by strange decay,
Their sinister faces lie;
The lid over each eye,
The grass and coloured clay
More motions have then they,
Joined to the great sunk silences.
Here is one not long dead;
His dark hearing caught our far wheels,
And the choked soul stretched weak hands
To reach the living word the far wheels said,
The blood-dazed intelligence beating for light,
Crying through the suspense of the far torturing wheels
Swift for the end to break,
Or the wheels to break,
Cried as the tide of the world broke over his sight.

Will they come? Will they ever come?
Even as the mixed hoofs of the mules,
The quivering-bellied mules,
And the rushing wheels all mixed
With his tortured upturned sight,

So we crashed round the bend,
We heard his weak scream,
We heard his very last sound,
And our wheels grazed his dead face.

Isaac Rosenberg

THE CENOTAPH

September 1919

Not yet will those measureless fields be green again
Where only yesterday the wild sweet blood of wonderful youth
    was shed;
There is a grave whose earth must hold too long, too deep a
    stain,
Though forever over it we may speak as proudly as we may
    tread.
But here, where the watchers by lonely hearths from the thrust
    of an inward sword have more slowly bled,
We shall build the Cenotaph: Victory, winged, with Peace,
    winged too, at the column's head.

And over the stairway, at the foot – oh! here, leave desolate,
    passionate hands to spread
Violets, roses, and laurel, with the small, sweet, tinkling country
    things
Speaking so wistfully of other Springs,
From the little gardens of little places where son or sweetheart
    was born and bred.
In splendid sleep, with a thousand brothers
             To lovers – to mothers
             Here, too, lies he:
 Under the purple, the green, the red,
 It is all young life: it must break some women's hearts to see
 Such a brave, gay coverlet to such a bed!
 Only, when all is done and said,
 God is not mocked and neither are the dead.
 For this will stand in our Market-place –
            Who'll sell, who'll buy
            (Will you or I
 Lie each to each with the better grace)?
 While looking into every busy whore's and huckster's face
 As they drive their bargains, is the Face
 Of God: and some young, piteous, murdered face.

Charlotte Mew

BIOGRAPHICAL NOTES

JOEL BARLOW (1754–1812) was born in Redding, Connecticut. He studied at Dartmouth College and Yale University. A politician and poet, he first came to public notice in 1778 with the publication of his anti-slavery poem, 'The Prospect of Peace'. He held diplomatic positions in Algeria and France. In this latter capacity, he was overcome by exposure during Napoleon's retreat from Moscow.

HAROLD BECKH (1894–1916) was born on New Year's Day in Great Amwell, Hertfordshire. He was educated at Cambridge and had intended on becoming a clergyman. During the First World War, he served in trenches near Bertrancourt, France. He was killed by machine gun fire while on patrol. A collection of Beckh's verse, *Swallows in Storm and Sunlight*, was published the following year.

AMBROSE BIERCE (1842–1914?) was born into a farming family near Horse Cave Creek, Ohio. During the American Civil War he served in the Union Army's 9th Indiana Infantry and fought at Shiloh, Murfreesboro, Chattanooga and Franklin. In June 1864, Bierce's wartime service ended after he received a head wound at the Battle of Kennesaw Mountain. Following the war, he embarked on a number of careers, the longest and most successful of which was as a newspaperman. In 1913, he left the United States to report on the Mexican Revolution. He was last heard from on December 26, 1913.

HORACE BRAY (1896–1918) was born in Thamesville, Ontario, and at the age of eighteen enlisted to fight in the First World War. A cavalryman, he was seriously wounded at Ypres. He recovered to become a second lieutenant in the Royal Air Force. He was killed in a collision at Shotwick, England.

RUPERT BROOKE (1887–1915) was born in Rugby, Warwickshire, where his father taught classics. A graduate of King's College, Cambridge, he was a familiar figure in literary and political circles. His first collection of verse, *Poems*, was published in 1911. He entered the First World War as a sub-lieutenant in the Royal Naval Division. While sailing the Aegean on the way to Gallipoli he died of acute blood poisoning, the result of a mosquito bite.

ELIZABETH BARRETT BROWNING (1806–1861) was born Elizabeth Barrett Moulton-Barrett at Croixhoe Hall, near Durham, England. Her first book, *The Battle of Marathon*, was published at the age of fourteen. An accomplished and popular poet, she was considered as a possible successor to William Wordsworth as England's poet laureate. She was married to the poet Robert Browning.

ROBERT BROWNING (1812–1889) was born in Camberwell, south London, the son of a clerk with the Bank of England. His education is said to have come primarily through his father's 6,000-volume private library. His first book, *Pauline: A Fragment of a Confession*, was published in 1833. He was married to the poet Elizabeth Barrett Browning.

ROBERT BURNS (1759–1796) was born in Alloway, South Ayrshire, Scotland, the son of a poor farming couple. Much of Burns' education came by way of his father, who supplemented his modest income through tutoring. In 1783 he began composing poetry employing the Ayrshire dialect. Three years later, the publication of his first collection, *Poems, Chiefly in the Scottish Dialect* (1786), established his reputation as national poet of Scotland.

THOMAS CAMPBELL (1777–1844) was born in Glasgow. Campbell studied at the University of Glasgow, where he received awards for his verse. Although he contemplated a career in law, the early success of his long poem, *The Pleasures of Hope* (1799), encouraged a life in letters. Campbell contributed to newspapers, magazines and encyclopedias, and served for more than a decade as editor of *The New Monthly Review*.

G. K. CHESTERTON (1874–1936) was born in Kensington, London. After studies at the Slade School of Art and University College London, he found work in publishing, supplementing his income as a freelance critic. Chesterton's first book, a collection of verse entitled *Greybeards at Play*, appeared in 1900.

He went on to produce well over 100 more titles, including novels, plays, biographies, essays and collections of short stories.

SAMUEL TAYLOR COLERIDGE (1772–1834) was born in Ottery St. Mary, Devonshire, the youngest of 16 children. Educated at Jesus College and Cambridge, as a poet, critic and philosopher, he was one of the key figures of the Romantic movement. Coleridge's impressive writing was both aided and hindered by an addiction to opium.

JOHN CORNFORD (1915–1936) was born in Cambridge to poets F. M. Cornford and Frances Darwin. While studying at Trinity College, Cambridge, he joined the Communist Party of Great Britain and left to fight in the Spanish Civil War as part of the International Brigade. He was killed at Lopera, a small city near Cordova. His body was never recovered.

LESLIE COULSON (1889–1916) was born at Kilburn. Before enlisting to serve in the First World War he was a well-known Fleet Street journalist. Coulson survived being wounded at Gallipoli in 1915, but died the following year at the Battle of the Somme. In 1917, a collection of his poetry, *From an Outpost and Other Poems*, became a bestseller in England.

STEPHEN CRANE (1871–1900) was born in Newark, New Jersey, the four-teenth child of a Methodist minister. As a youth, he wrote for *The New York Tribune* and other newspapers closer to home. Crane was expelled from both Lafayette College and Syracuse University, after which he moved to New York and began a career as a freelance writer. He is best remembered for *The Red Badge of Courage*, the great novel of the American Civil War.

T. W. H. CROSLAND (1865–1924) was born in Leeds. An outspoken Tory journalist, he served as critic and editor for a number of Fleet Street publications. He published several volumes of poetry, including *War Poems by X* (1916). His collected poems, published in 1917, was followed by the posthumous *Last Poems* (1928).

WILLIAM DAVENANT (1606–1668) is thought to have been born in Oxford. The godson of William Shakespeare, it was rumoured that the bard was his biological father. Davenant studied at Oxford, but left before earning a degree. In 1637 he was made Poet Laureate. Though a supporter of Charles I during the English Civil War, Davenant was later knighted and served the Crown in France and the colonies of Virginia and Maryland. Largely a writer involved in the stage, his *The Siege of Rhodes*, first performed in 1656, is considered the first English opera.

EMILY DICKINSON (1832–1886) was born in Amherst, Massachusetts, where she led a reclusive and eccentric life. Though she is today considered one of the great American poets, only seven of her 1,800-odd poems saw print during her lifetime. The first collection of Dickinson's verse, *Poems*, was published four years after her death.

JOHN DONNE (1572–1631) was born in London. Educated at Oxford and Cambridge, he served as a Member of Parliament. In his later years, he was ordained into the Church of England, eventually serving as Dean in London's St. Paul's Cathedral. Donne's first collection of verse, *Poems*, was published two years after his death.

KEITH DOUGLAS (1920–1944) was born in Tunbridge Wells, Kent, the son of a retired army captain. Financial hardship, combined with an unwell mother and the eventual collapse of his parents' marriage, made for a trying childhood. Douglas attended Oxford on scholarship, where he was tutored by the poet Edmund Blunden. He enlisted just days after the start of the Second World War, serving most of his time in the Middle East and North Africa. At the end of 1943, Douglas returned to England, and, in June 1944, he took part in the D-Day invasion of Normandy. Three days later, he was killed by mortar fire outside Bayeux.

MICHAEL DRAYTON (1563–1631) was born near Nuneaton, Warwickshire. Though a prominent poet of the Elizabethan era, little is known about his early life. He was much published, beginning in 1591 with *The Harmony of the Church*, a volume of verse. Though the main body of his work is composed of poetry, Drayton was for a time employed as a playwright. He was a friend of Ben Jonson, who contributed the lines placed over his grave in Westminster Abbey.

EBENEZER ELLIOTT (1781–1849), the 'Corn Law Rhymer', was born into a strict Calvinist family in Masbrough, Yorkshire. Largely self-educated, he married in 1806 and had thirteen children, though he suffered from ill-health for much of his life. Much of Elliott's verse is consumed by radical politics and his opposition to British Corn Laws, as expressed in *The Ranter* (1830) and *Corn Law Rhymes* (1831).

RALPH WALDO EMERSON (1803–1882) was born in Boston. After attending Harvard, he worked as an educator, and later became a Unitarian clergyman like his father. In 1832, having determined the ministry 'antiquated', he resigned from the church. An essayist and poet, Emerson derived much of his income through his considerable skill as a public orator. His books often grew out of his lectures. Three collections of poetry, *Poems* (1847), *May-Day and Other Pieces* (1867), and *Selected Poems* (1876), were published during his lifetime.

FRANCIS MILES FINCH (1827–1907) was born in Ithica, New York. A Yale graduate, he practised law, served on the bench, and lectured at Cornell University, an institution he had helped establish. A collection of his poetry, *The Blue and the Gray, and Other Verses* (1909) was published posthumously.

GEORGE GORDON, LORD BYRON (1788–1824) was born in London. At the age of ten he inherited the title and estates of his great-uncle, the 5th Baron Byron. In 1806, the year after he began studies at Cambridge, he published *Fugitive Pieces*, his first collection of verse. A prolific poet and one of the leading figures in the Romantic movement, his accomplished works are often overshadowed by an extravagant life of scandal, intrigue and sexual adventure.

JULIAN GRENFELL (1888–1915), the eldest son of the Earl of Desborough, was born in London. He was educated at Eton and Oxford and, in 1910, joined the Royal Dragoons. A recipient of the Distinguished Service Order in 1914, in the First World War Grenfell was hit by shrapnel during the Second Battle of Ypres. He succumbed to his wounds four weeks later, aged 27.

IVOR GURNEY (1890–1937) was born in Gloucester. A talented youth, at the age of 14 he began composing both music and verse. Gurney was studying at the Royal College of Music at the start of the First World War. He enlisted as a private, and in 1917 was wounded and gassed. Gurney's wartime experience inspired two volumes of verse, *Severn and Somme* (1917) and *War's Embers* (1919). Gurney suffered from untreated bipolar illness and, in 1922, began the first of his final fifteen years in mental hospitals.

THOMAS HARDY (1840–1928) was born in Higher Bockhampton, Dorset. The son of a stonemason, he trained as an architect and moved to London where he was awarded prizes from the Royal Institute of British Architects and the Architectural Association. The author of several classic novels, including *Far from the Madding Crowd* (1874), *Tess of the d'Urbervilles* (1891) and *Jude the Obscure* (1895), Hardy turned his talents increasingly toward verse in later life.

W. S. HAWKINS (1837–1865) was born in Madison County, Alabama. A student at the outbreak of the American Civil War, he enlisted and quickly rose to the rank of colonel. In January 1864 Hawkins was captured and imprisoned for the remainder of the conflict. He died mere months after his release.

A. E. HOUSMAN (1859–1936) was born in Worcestershire. Awarded a scholarship to Oxford, he studied classics. The brother of writers Laurence and Clemence, for most of his life he taught Latin at Cambridge. His masterpiece, *The Shropshire Lad* (1896), was rejected by several publishers and was eventually published at his own expense. Housman's war poetry was influenced by the death of his brother Herbert during the Boer Wars.

HENRY HOWARD, EARL OF SURREY (1517–1547) began life in Hunsdon, Hertfordshire, the son of the future Duke of Norfolk. Born of royal blood, he was raised with Henry Fitzroy, the illegitimate son of Henry VIII. Upon the death of his grandfather in 1524, Howard became the Earl of Surrey. A cousin to Anne Boleyn, Howard was accused – most probably falsely – of planning to usurp the crown, and was beheaded.

JULIA WARD HOWE (1819–1910) was born in New York City. At 23, she married physician Samuel Gridley Howe, a fellow abolitionist and educator. A prolific travel writer, playwright, and poet, Howe is best remembered for her anthem 'The Battle Hymn of the Republic'. The song, first published in 1862 edition, was one of the most popular of the American Civil War. Howe is also credited with the creation of Mother's Day, through her 1870 Mother's Day Proclamation.

JOHN KEATS (1795–1821) was born in London, the son of a hostler. Apprenticed to a surgeon, he later studied literature at Guy's Hospital. His first volume of verse, *Poems* (1817), was poorly received. Four years later, he died of tuberculosis while visiting Italy. Not long after his death, he became recognized as one of the great poets of the English Romantic movement.

T. M. KETTLE (1880–1916) was born in Artane, County Dublin. A Member of Parliament, lawyer, professor and journalist, he was an advocate for Irish home rule. He enlisted not long after the start of the First World War and was killed at the Battle of the Somme. In 1917 his wartime writing was collected in the volume *The Ways of War*.

FRANCIS SCOTT KEY (1779–1843) was born at his family's plantation in Frederick Country (Carroll County), Maryland. He studied law at St. John's College, Annapolis. During the War of 1812, he witnessed the Battle of Baltimore, which inspired his patriotic poem 'The Defence of Fort Henry'. Set to music, as 'The Star Spangled Banner', it was adopted as the national anthem of the United States in 1915. The first collection of Key's poetry was published fourteen years after his death.

RUDYARD KIPLING (1865–1936) was born in Bombay (Mumbai), India to English parents. Accomplished in many genres, he is best remembered today for his children's writing, *The Jungle Book* (1894), *The Second Jungle Book* (1895) and *Just So Stories* (1902). Kipling wrote two collections of poetry, *Barrack-Room Ballads and Other Verses* (1893) and *Rudyard Kipling's Verse* (1923).

YUSEF KOMUNYAKAA (1947–) was born James Willie Brown, Jr. in Bogalusa, Louisiana. From 1965 to 1967 he served in the United States Army and did a tour of duty in South Vietnam. He studied at the University of Colorado, Colorado State University and the University of California, Irvine. Komunyakaa has written over a dozen books of poetry, including *Dien Cai Dau* (1988), which focuses on his experiences during the Vietnam War.

D. H. LAWRENCE (1885–1930) was born in Eastwood, Nottinghamshire. He studied at University College, Nottingham, where he earned a teaching certificate. In 1913 Lawrence published his first volume of verse, *Love Poems and Others*. A key figure in 20th-century literature, he is best remembered for the novel *Lady Chatterley's Lover* (1928), which was a frequent target of censors.

ALUN LEWIS (1915–1944) was born in Cwmaman, Wales. He studied at the University College of Wales, Aberystwyth (now University of Aberystwyth) and the University of Manchester, and worked briefly as a teacher. Though a pacifist, in 1940 Lewis joined the Royal Engineers, and later served in the Education Corps. Lewis published two books while in service, a collection of stories titled *The Last Inspection* (1942) and *Raider's Dawn and other poems* (1942). His death from a self-inflicted gunshot wound at India's Goppa Pass was determined to have been the result of an accident.

HENRY WADSWORTH LONGFELLOW (1807–1882) was born in Portland, Maine. He was educated at Bowdoin College in Brunswick, where he became a professor. After accepting an appointment at Harvard, he relocated to Cambridge, Massachusetts. Longfellow was the most famous and well-loved American poet of his day. An ardent abolitionist, Longfellow's writing on the American Civil War, was overshadowed by the horrific death of his second wife, from burns suffered in a fire, in the second month of the conflict.

RICHARD LOVELACE (1618–1659) is thought to have been born in Woolwich, Kent. He attended Oxford, where he first began composing verse. Later, during studies at Cambridge, Lovelace became involved in politics, an effort that would twice lead to imprisonment. In 1649 he published his only book of verse, *Lucasta: Epodes, Odes, Sonnets, Songs, etc.* Once a wealthy man, he lived his final years in poverty and ill-health.

DANIEL BEDINGER LUCAS (1836–1909) was born in Charlestown, Virginia (now West Virginia). The son of a congressman, he attended the University of Virginia, and later practised law. During the American Civil War he served on the staff of Confederate General Henry A. Wise. After the war, Lucas returned to law and was appointed to the West Virginia Supreme Court of Appeals. An adept politician, he was elected to the State Legislature and the United States Senate. Among his books are *The Wreath of Eglantine and Other Poems* (1869) and *The Maid of Northumberland* (1879), a verse play set during the Civil War.

W. S. S. LYON (1886–1915) joined the Royal Scots the year before the outbreak of the First World War. He served in France and Belgium and was killed by shellfire near Ypres. A collection of verse, *Easter at Ypres 1915 and Other Poems*, was published posthumously.

THOMAS BABINGTON MACAULAY (1800–1859) was born in Rothley Temple, Leicestershire, the son of abolitionist Zachary Macaulay. He was first recognized for his poetry while studying at Cambridge. As a young man, Macaulay embarked on a political career that would see him as Secretary at War. While his political fortunes were mixed, he enjoyed great popularity as a historian and writer of historical verse.

HAMISH MANN was the pseudonym of ARTHUR JAMES MANN (1896–1917). He was born in Broughty Ferry, Forfarshire, and was educated in Edinburgh. In 1915, he enlisted to fight in the First World War. A veteran of the Battle of the Somme, he was wounded at Arras and died the following day. A collection of Mann's war poetry, *A Subaltern's Musings*, was published the year after his death.

ANDREW MARVELL (1621–1678) was born in Winestead-in-Holderness, East Yorkshire, the son of a clergyman. He attended Cambridge and served many years as a Member of Parliament. A supporter of Oliver Crowell, after the restoration he was obliged to publish much of his writing anonymously.

KATHERINE MANSFIELD (1888–1923) was born Katherine Mansfield Beauchamp in Wellington, New Zealand. She studied at Queen's College,

London, during which time she began to write sketches and prose poems. Although she returned to New Zealand, much of her life was spent moving amongst the literary circles of Europe. Her debut collection of verse, *Poems*, was published in the year of her death.

JOHN McCRAE (1872–1918) was born in Guelph, Ontario. He studied medicine at the University of Toronto, finishing at the top of his class. In 1899, he was awarded a fellowship in pathology at McGill University, but delayed further study to serve in the Boer War. A lieutenant-colonel, he served the greater part of the First World War as a surgeon at the Front and at a hospital in Boulogne, where he died of pneumonia complicated by meningitis. His only collection of verse, *In Flanders Fields and Other Poems*, was published a year after his death.

HERMAN MELVILLE (1819–1891) was born in New York City. His education was disrupted several times by bankruptcy and the death of his father. As an adult, Melville worked as a sailor and a schoolteacher. His experiences as the former served to inspire the majority of his novels. Melville's early work was quite popular, but his audience quickly declined. *Moby-Dick* (1851), his masterpiece, was a commercial failure. Melville's first collection of poetry, *Battle-Pieces and Aspects of the War: Civil War Poems* (1866), sold fewer than 500 copies. In later life, he turned to public speaking and, for nearly two decades, worked as a customs inspector for the City of New York.

GEORGE MEREDITH (1828–1909) was born in Portsmouth, England. He studied law, but ultimately chose to pursue a career in journalism. Although best remembered as the author of *The Egoist* (1879), the most accomplished of his 19 novels, Meredith published nine volumes of verse, beginning with *Poems* (1851).

CHARLOTTE MEW (1869–1928) was born in Bloomsbury, London. Her first published work, the short story 'Passed', appeared in an 1894 issue of *The Yellow Book*. Mew's first collection of verse, a chapbook entitled *The Farmer's Bride*, was published in 1916. A member of a family that struggled with mental illness, she took her own life.

JOHN MILTON (1608–1674) was born in London, the son of a Puritan composer. He studied at Cambridge, during which time he wrote much of his finest poetry. His first known published poem, 'On Shakespear', appeared anonymously in the 1632 Second Folio edition of the playwright's works. Milton's masterpiece, the epic poem *Paradise Lost*, was published in 1667.

SIR HENRY NEWBOLT (1862–1938) was born in Bilston, Wolverhampton, the son of a clergyman. He attended Oxford and was later called to the bar. Newbolt's first book, the novel *Taken from the Enemy* (1892), was followed by the tragedy *Modred* (1895), but it was verse that established his literary reputation. His 'Vitaï Lampada' was used for propaganda purposes during the First World War.

THOMAS LOVE PEACOCK (1785–1866) was born in Melcombe Regis (Weymouth), Dorset. Aged sixteen he moved to London, taking up independent study at the British Museum. His first collection of verse, *The Monks of St Mark* (1804), was self-published. Though employed for much of his life by the British East India Company, Peacock managed to produce twenty volumes, including novels, poetry and essays.

WILFRED OWEN (1893–1918) was born in Ostwestry, Shropshire. Educated at the Birkenhead Institute and the University of London, he was teaching abroad when the First World War broke out. In 1915 he returned to England in order to enlist. In May 1917, while serving in the trenches in France, he was caught in an explosion. Diagnosed with shellshock, he was sent to England in order to recover. Owen returned to France in August 1918, and was awarded the Military Cross two months later. On November 4, 1918, he was killed by German machine gun fire. The first collection of his verse, *Poems* (1920), was edited by his friend Siegfried Sassoon.

GEORGE PEELE (*c.*1556–1596) was born in London and educated at Christ's Hospital and Oxford. A poet and translator best remembered for his drama *Edward I*, he is thought by some to have contributed to *Titus Andronicus*. Peele's reputation as a reckless soul is reflected in the commonly held belief that he died 'of the pox'.

AUGUSTUS JULIAN REQUIER (1825–1887) was born in Charleston, South Carolina, the son of French and Haitian parents. Requier's first book, *The Spanish Exile* (1842), a play in blank verse, was published at the age of seventeen. Two years later, he was admitted to the bar. In 1853, Requier was appointed United States district attorney, and held the equivalent position under the Confederate government during the American Civil War. After the conflict, he relocated in New York City and became active in municipal politics.

ALEXANDER ROBERTSON (1882–1916) was born in Edinburgh. An academic, he wrote several books, including a biography, *The Life of Robert Moray*. He was killed on the first day of the Battle of the Somme. A collection, *The Last Poems of Alexander Robertson*, was published in 1918.

ISAAC ROSENBERG (1890–1918) was born in Bristol to Russian immigrants. Though a talented poet – his first collection of verse, *Night and Day*, was published in 1912 – he considered himself a portrait artist. He was in South Africa when the First World War began. He returned to England to enlist and was killed in close combat near the French village of Fampoux. The first collection of his verse, *Poems*, was published in 1922.

ABRAM JOSEPH RYAN (1839–1886) was born in Norfolk, Virginia. The son of Irish immigrants, he became a Roman Catholic priest and served as a chaplain in the Confederate Army during the American Civil War. After the conflict, Ryan founded *The Banner of the South*, a religious and political weekly. His writings were published in several volumes, the most popular being *Poems: Patriotic, Religious, and Miscellaneous* (1880).

CHARLES SACKVILLE (1638–1706) was a poet and rake. The son of nobility, he inherited vast estates and in 1677 succeeded his father as Earl of Dorset. Sackville is perhaps best remembered for his song 'To All You Ladies Now at Land'. He was a great patron of the arts, and helped support John Dryden, amongst others.

H. SMALLEY SARSON (1890–unknown) was born in London, England. A farmer, at the beginning of the First World War he enlisted in the Canadian

Expeditionary Force. Sarson wrote a single volume of verse, *From Field and Hospital* (1916).

CHARLES SANGSTER (1822–1893) was born in Kingston, Upper Canada (Ontario). As a young man, he held a variety of newspaper positions before settling into a career in mid-life with the Ottawa Post Office. Two volumes of verse, *The St. Lawrence and the Saguenay and Other Poems* (1856) and *Hesperus and Other Poems and Lyrics* (1860), were published during his lifetime.

SIEGFRIED SASSOON (1886–1967) was born to a wealthy family in Matfield, Kent. He studied law and history at Cambridge, but left before taking a degree. His first book, a verse parody entitled *The Daffodil Murderer* (1913), was published under the pseudonym 'Saul Kain'. Sassoon enlisted in the militia in the run up to the First World War, was twice wounded and suffered the loss of a brother at Gallipoli. Known for his bravery, after speaking out against the conflict, he was removed from service and treated for shellshock. During his convalescence, he met and served as a mentor to Wilfred Owen. A prolific writer, after the war Sassoon published over 30 volumes of verse and prose, including a biography of George Meredith.

JOHN SCOTT (1731–1783), often referred to as JOHN SCOTT OF AMWELL, was a poet from Hertfordshire. Born in Southwark to a wealthy Quaker couple, he was noted for his pastoral verse. Scott's *Poetical Works* was published the year before his death.

ALAN SEEGER (1888–1916) was born in New York and spent much of his childhood in Mexico. Educated at Harvard, for several years he lived a bohemian lifestyle in Greenwich Village. He was visiting London, conducting research at the British Museum, when the First World War began. Seeger joined the French Foreign Legion and was killed in France at Belloy-en-Santerre. A collection of verse, *Poems*, was published a few months after his death.

HENRY LAMONT SIMPSON (1897–1918) was born in Crosby-on-Eden, Carlisle. A student at Cambridge, he become a commissioned officer in

1917. He was killed by a sniper at Strazeele, France. His only collection of poetry, *Moods and Tenses*, was published the year after the war ended.

CHARLES HAMILTON SORLEY (1895–1915) was born in Aberdeen, the son of a university professor. After winning a scholarship, he attended Oxford. He enlisted in 1914 and, less than a year later, was commissioned as a captain. He was killed by a sniper at the Battle of Loos. A collection of verse, *Marlborough and Other Poems*, was published the year after his death.

ROBERT SOUTHEY (1774–1843) was born in Bristol. Educated at Oxford, his first major work, the play *The Fall of Robespierre*, was composed before the age of twenty. Southey was a prolific poet, novelist, essayist and travel writer. Although he held the position of Poet Laureate for three decades, he is best remembered for the story of 'Goldilocks and the Three Bears', which first saw print in his novel *The Doctor* (1834).

CHARLES ALGERNON SWINBURNE (1837–1909) was born in London. A graduate of Eton and Oxford, he was one of England's foremost Decadent poets. Though he at times courted controversy, Swinburne's talent led to speculation that he might one day be Poet Laureate.

E. WYNDHAM TENNANT (1897–1916) was born in Wiltshire, the son of Baron Glenconnor. His younger brother was the great aesthete Stephen Tennant. A 17-year-old schoolboy, he enlisted at the beginning of the First World War. Tennant was killed by a sniper's bullet at the Battle of the Somme. His first collection of verse, *Worple Flit and Other Poems*, was published the year of his death.

ALFRED, LORD TENNYSON (1809–1892) was born in Somersby, Lincolnshire, the son of a clergyman and one of 11 children. He was educated at Cambridge, during which time his first book, *Poems, Chiefly Lyrical* (1830), was published. With the death of his father the following spring, he was forced to abandon his studies. In 1850 Tennyson was made Poet Laureate, a position he held until his death. His remains the longest tenure in the position.

EDWARD THOMAS (1878–1917) was born in London to Welsh parents. He studied at Oxford on a history scholarship. In 1899 he married the daughter of James Ashcroft Noble, an eighteenth-century literary figure. Encouraged by his father-in-law, Thomas pursued a life in letters as an author, editor and reviewer. His first poems were written in 1914, the year before he enlisted to fight in the First World War. Thomas was killed by a shell at Arras. Several collections of his verse were published in the years immediately following his death.

JAMES THOMSON (1700–1748), the son of a Presbyterian minister, was born at Ednam, Roxburghshire. He studied at the College of Edinburgh, where he became a member of a literary group known as the Grotesque Club. Thomson wrote a number of poems, including *The Seasons* (1730), but is best remembered for 'Rule, Britannia', which was set to music by James Arne in 1740.

HENRY TIMROD (1829–1867), the 'Poet of the Confederacy', was born in Charleston, South Carolina. The son of a minor poet, his first collection of verse, *Poems*, was published in 1860. The younger Timrod worked as a tutor and as a journalist and editor for a number of newspapers, most notably *The Daily South Carolinian*. Reduced to poverty when his home was destroyed during the American Civil War, he died of tuberculosis two years after the fighting ceased.

BERNARD FREEMAN TROTTER (1890–1917) was born at Toronto and spent much of his youth in Wolfville, Nova Scotia. Though his initial attempt to enlist during the First World War was thwarted by ill-health, he finally set sail for Europe in March 1916. A little over a year later, Trotter was killed by a shell while serving as a Transport Officer at the Front. His only collection of poems, *A Canadian Twilight and other Poems of War and of Peace*, was published in the month of the Armistice.

BRIAN TURNER (1967–) was born in Visalia, California, He studied at California State University, Fresno and the University of Oregon. Turner served with the United States Army in Bosnia and Herzegovina and Iraq. His first book, *Here, Bullet*, a collection of war poems, was published in 2005.

EDGAR WALLACE (1875–1932) was born in Greenwich, London, the son of an unwed actress. Adopted by a working-class couple, at the age of eleven he began his working life by selling newspapers. He served in the medical staff corps during the Boer War, an experience that inspired a number of works including *The Mission that Failed!* (1898) and *Writ in Barracks* (1900). After leaving the military, Wallace turned to writing. One of the most prolific writers in the English language, he is credited with 175 novels. His best known creation is 'King Kong'.

ARTHUR GRAEME WEST (1891–1917) was born in Norfolk and spent his childhood in London. He was educated at Oxford and in 1915 enlisted to serve in the First World War. West quickly rose in the ranks to captain before being killed by a sniper outside Bapaume, France. *The Diary of a Dead Officer*, containing poems, essays and extracts from his journal, was published in 1919.

WALT WHITMAN (1819–1892) was born in West Hills, New York. After leaving school he undertook a variety of occupations, including printer, carpenter, teacher and newspaper editor. Whitman's key work *Leaves of Grass* first appeared in 1855 as a slim of twelve poems. He spent much of the remainder of his life revising the work, adding and, on occasion, removing verse. The last edition, published the year before his death, included nearly 400 poems. In 1862, after his brother, George Washington Whitman, was wounded in Fredericksburg, Virginia, Whitman volunteered as an army nurse and ministered to soldiers in Washington. He recorded his war-time experiences in *Drum-Taps* (1865) and *Memoranda During the War* (1867).

JOHN GREENLEAF WHITTIER (1807–1892) was born in Haverhill, Massachusetts. He received little in the way of formal education, yet made his literary debut at the age of nineteen. A dedicated abolitionist, Whittier entered politics and promoted the cause through his editorship of a number of influential periodicals. He turned from politics after the Civil War and dedicated himself completely to poetry. In his time, Whittier was considered one of the great American poets, second only to Henry Wadsworth Longfellow.

CHARLES WOLFE (1791–1823) was born in Blackhall, Ireland, and lived much of his early life in England. He studied at Trinity College, Dublin and was ordained as a minister in the Church of Ireland. His only volume of verse, *Poetical Remains*, appeared two years after his death from tuberculosis.

WILLIAM WORDSWORTH (1770–1850) was born in Cockermouth on the River Derwent, England. He completed his studies at Cambridge in 1791, and two years later published his first two volumes of verse, *An Evening Walk* and *Descriptive Sketches*. With his friend, Samuel Taylor Coleridge, he is credited with launching the Romantic movement in English literature. Wordsworth was made Poet Laureate in 1843, a position he held until his death.

W. B. YEATS (1865–1939) was born in Sandymount, Ireland, the son of a lawyer and portrait painter. He was educated in Dublin and London, where he became an important fixture in literary circles. A poet, playwright and writer of folklore, Yeats' first collection book, a verse play entitled *Mosada*, was published in 1886. Though Yeats was awarded the 1923 Nobel Prize in Literature, chiefly for his work as a playwright, he is today celebrated more for his poetry.

INDEX OF POETS

INDEX OF TITLES

INDEX OF FIRST LINES